THOUGHT CHOICE POWER

Charting the Course of Liberty in Modern Society

Human nature itself is evermore an advocate for liberty. There is also in human nature a resentment of injury and indignation against wrong; a love of truth, and a veneration for virtue.

– John Adams, Novanglus Essay No. I

Plebeius

Plebeian Publishing Company

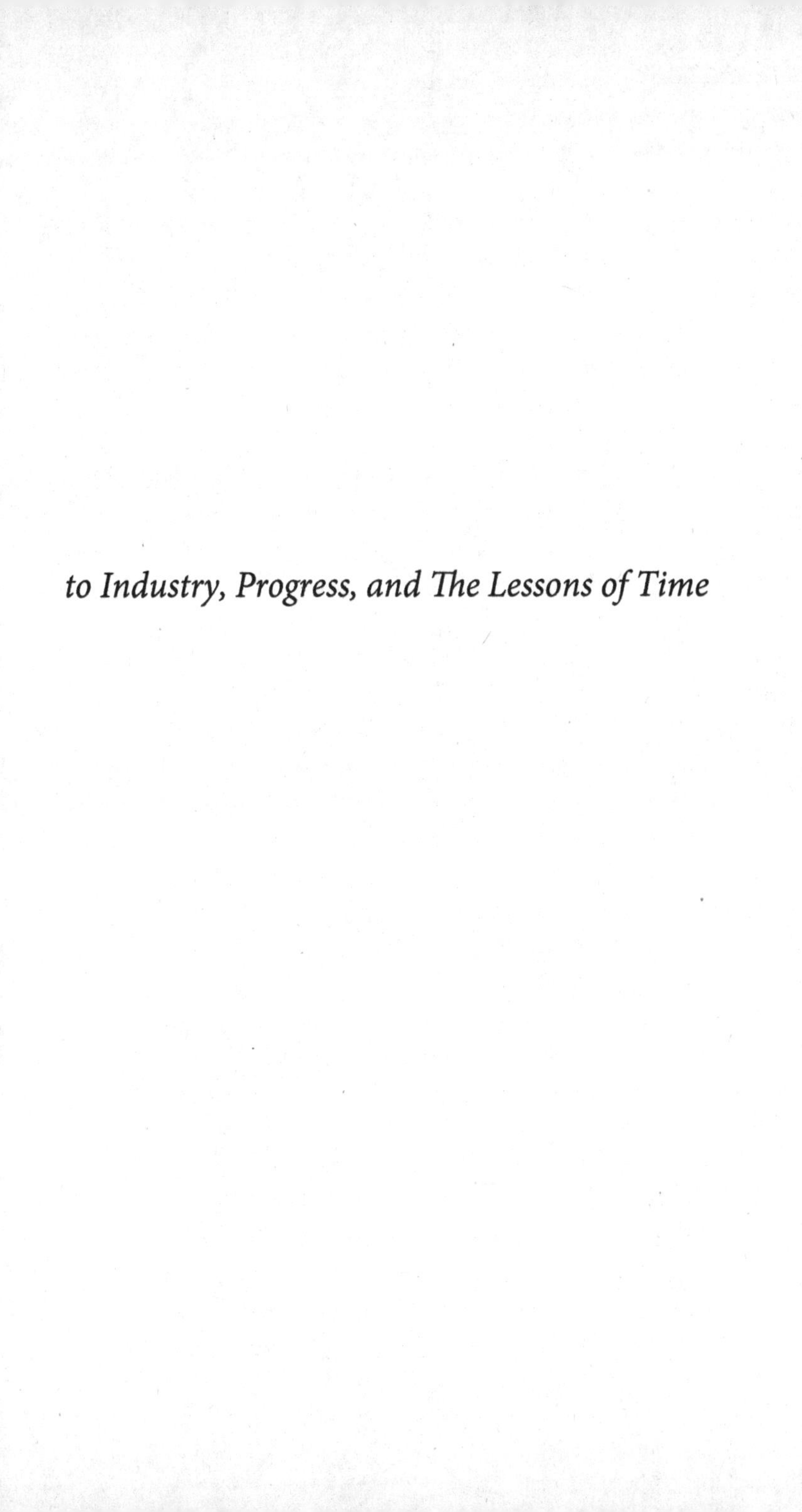

to Industry, Progress, and The Lessons of Time

The abridged excerpt below is from Novanglus Essay No. I – John Adams' 1775 rebuttal to the argument against revolution as put forth by the anonymous writer Massachusettensis. These words of Adams, along with the unease of our day, involve Massachusettensis' assertion that "There is a latent spark in the breasts of the people, capable of being kindled into a flame, and to do this has always been the employment of the disaffected."

We have much to learn from history.

My Friends,—

A writer, under the signature of Massachusettensis, has addressed you, in a series of papers, on the great national subject of the present quarrel between the British administration and the Colonies. As I have not in my possession more than one of his essays, and that is in the Gazette of December 26, I will take the liberty, in the spirit of candor and decency, to bespeak your attention upon the same subject.

There may be occasion to say very severe things, before I shall have finished what I propose, in opposition to this writer, but there ought to be no reviling. Rem ipsam dic, mitte male loqui, which may be justly translated, speak out the whole truth boldly, but use no bad language...

"There is a latent spark in the breasts of the people, capable of being kindled into a flame, and to do this has always been the employment

of the disaffected." What is this latent spark? The love of liberty. A Deo hominis est indita naturae. Human nature itself is evermore an advocate for liberty. There is also in human nature a resentment of injury and indignation against wrong; a love of truth, and a veneration for virtue. These amiable passions are the "latent spark" to which those whom this writer calls the "disaffected" apply. If the people are capable of understanding, seeing, and feeling the difference between true and false, right and wrong, virtue and vice, to what better principle can the friends of mankind apply, than to the sense of this difference? Is it better to apply, as this writer and his friends do, to the basest passions in the human breast—to their fear, their vanity, their avarice, ambition, and every kind of corruption? I appeal to all experience, and to universal history, if it has ever been in the power of popular leaders, uninvested with other authority than what is conferred by the popular suffrage, to persuade a large people, for any length of time together, to think themselves wronged, injured, and oppressed, unless they really were, and saw and felt it to be so.

"They," the popular leaders, "begin by reminding the people of the elevated rank they hold in the universe, as men; that all men by nature are equal; that kings are but the ministers of the people; that their authority is delegated to them by the people, for their good, and they have a right

to resume it, and place it in other hands, or keep it themselves, whenever it is made use of to oppress them. Doubtless, there have been instances when these principles have been inculcated to obtain a redress of real grievances; but they have been much oftener perverted to the worst of purposes."

These are what are called revolution principles. They are the principles of Aristotle and Plato, of Livy and Cicero, and Sidney, Harrington, and Locke; the principles of nature and eternal reason; the principles on which the whole government over us now stands. It is therefore astonishing, if any thing can be so, that writers, who call themselves friends of government, should in this age and country be so inconsistent with themselves, so indiscreet, so immodest, as to insinuate a doubt concerning them...[i]

---

i "I. To the Inhabitants of the Colony of Massachusetts-Bay, 23 January 1775," *Founders Online*, National Archives, https://founders.archives.gov/documents/Adams/06-02-02-0072-0002. [Original source: *The Adams Papers*, Papers of John Adams, vol. 2, *December 1773–April 1775*, ed. Robert J. Taylor. Cambridge, MA: Harvard University Press, 1977, pp. 226–233.]

Contents

Preface

Ten words and a question mark. Ten simple words that probably should have been five. I completely underestimated the perception-altering power of the question and its requirements. All I did was ask myself, "What makes us, us Americans, a single entity, a Nation?" I guess I didn't appreciate just how conflicted a protagonist We, the People, truly are, never mind the hours it would take to answer the question honestly.

The question came to mind during the latter part of September 2008, shortly after a few small business employees asked if I could explain what was causing our little worlds to meltdown. Unsurprisingly, my attempt to answer their question, to explain – Bretton Woods and its demise, Glass-Steagall and its repeal, fractional lending, collateralized debt obligations, and Credit Default Swaps, each alongside a brief synopsis of Laissez-faire – was mostly inadequate. In fact, we were no better off until I pulled from the pocket of my blue jeans the cash and coin I had – $1.54, or thereabouts – placing the money on the workbench between us while asking, "How much is this worth?" Only when one of the guys sheepishly said, "$1.54", to which I responded, "No, WHAT is it really worth?", did we begin to understand our problem and how far our reality was from our control.

Not long after that, a real sense of disgust set in, and I started to wonder what my country's founders might think of our situation. A few days later, I typed my question at the top of a page and then began to search the words of George Washington and his contemporaries.

I don't know why I was compelled to type the question. A fleeting utterance should have been enough. Nevertheless, a list of quotations soon took shape – the passages at first limited to the earliest Presidents, only to be quickly expanded to include many of those generally considered to be within the historical Top 20. Presidents so recent that present-day passions would likely interfere were excluded.

Once the quotes were categorized, it was clear that (a) my question of nation had opened the doors to many more questions, most of which led to countless others, et cetera, (b) there were specific topics repeated to a level of supreme importance, (c) the nature of our problem is by no means limited to the United States or this moment in history – it is an ageless problem shared by all ordinary people, and (d) it would take some time to answer my question. With no real aim, I began to uncover the interconnectedness of our existence as well as the nature of the dangers before us, and I began to write.

Looking back, I should have realized that my question was not so simple and that an honest inquiry would point me toward humanity's inescapable theme of Liberty and Justice for All. I should have been able to see through the fog of our predicament, or at least deep enough into it to know that my inquiry would require an exploration of the thickened plot that we call Happiness.

When the initial question first came to mind, my goal was to improve my understanding of the day's events in a broad contextual sense so that I might make better decisions. I did not know that my question, if I was willing to persist, was an inquiry capable of illuminating an entire complex of wisdom. I had no idea that a moving portrait would appear – an image of from where we have come and to where we are headed – and that my self-help inquiry would turn into a proverbial labor of love.

In short, it was a search for better personal outcomes that led me to history and the interconnected nature of our reality, to responsibility and the precepts of care and prudence, to reconciliation and the middle points of life, to opportunity, to dysfunction and ignorance and the status quo, to antagonists in search of control, and to leadership.

Before closing this preface, my sincerest thanks to those of you who took the time to read rough drafts or earlier versions of this work. Your contribution was invaluable, and I am sorry if you scratched your head raw. I know it was an uncomfortable experience.

Lastly, a few definitions and expectations must be stated before proceeding to the work. Please consider the following eight points:

(1) As an escaped slave turned statesman, writer, orator, and abolitionist, Frederick Douglass believed we should uphold the principles of "the fathers of this republic" instead of discounting their wisdom because of their many deeply flawed choices. His perspective is a valuable example of reconciling right and wrong within the historical record. The following words of Douglass constitute the underpinnings of both wisdom and progress:

> *Fellow Citizens, I am not wanting in respect for the fathers of this republic. The signers of the Declaration of Independence were brave men. They were great men too – great enough to give fame to a great age. It does not often happen to a nation to raise, at one time, such a number of truly great men. The point from which I am compelled to view them is not, certainly the most favorable; and yet I cannot contemplate their great deeds with less than admiration. They were statesmen, patriots and heroes, and for the good they did, and the principles they contended for, I will unite with you to honor their memory.*

(2) The timelessness of Injustice the world over, of the economic and the social struggles faced by all peoples in all lands, is no better illuminated than by these words of Abraham Lincoln, referenced in chapter XVIII, *In Response*:

> *…the real issue… is the issue that will continue in this country when these poor tongues of Judge Douglas and myself shall be silent. It is the eternal struggle between these two principles – right and wrong – throughout the world. They are the two principles that have stood face to face from the beginning of time, and will ever continue to struggle. The one is the common right of humanity and the other the divine right of kings. It is the same principle in whatever shape it develops itself. It is the same spirit that says, 'You work and toil and earn bread, and I'll eat it.' No matter in what shape it comes, whether from the mouth of a king who seeks to bestride the people of his own nation and live by the fruit of their labor, or from one race of men as an apology for enslaving another race, it is the same tyrannical principle.*

(3) So as not to be misunderstood, our often-mentioned Monied Interests are no more uniform in their actions than are We, the People. Therefore, it is the greater part with which we are primarily concerned, as stated in chapter XI, *Virtuous Cycles of Endeavor*:

A majority of the Monied Interests and their merchants seek to manipulate our System for their own gain – they do not possess a Care about our endeavors or our "general Welfare." They have been proven to be unconcerned with the "Posterity" of anyone but themselves and their lineage. It is ultimately the deal; the bigger, the better – their satisfying sale of anything inflated regardless of locale and irrespective of tangibility – that is their sole concern.

Also, our definition of the Monied Interests is as plainly expressed in chapter XIV, *In Good Faith*:

The Monied Interests, devoted as they are to that which they in their minds so richly deserve – all those possessing little respect for any balance aside from that of their ledgers – they see us as barely more than numbers to be plied per their desires, debits and credits alike.

The Monied Interests, with their many offspring in tow – all those of this world far less concerned with the things that must be good in as much as they are focused upon advancing their positions and acquiring their next measure of Power – they are why We can no longer afford to bite our tongues and pray for a better day.

(4) As far as we can see, history is close to linear; our reality is far from it. Therefore, this work could not be arranged in a simple, direct construct. Ideas and topics could not be neatly contained within a single chapter or line of consecutive chapters. This, our reality, is stated early on, in chapter II, *A Large Fleet*:

...the equation of life these days has come to be increasingly highlighted by relationships entwined and connections layered, a reality folded many times over with threads all through.

Thus, the three "parts" – Thought, Choice, Power – are sequentially stacked. If I've done my job well, you will recognize ideas and topics as well as threads related to our problems, their investigation, and our solutions, woven throughout in Fibonacci-inspired sequences.

(5) There is a nautical theme to this work, appropriate on several levels and predicated on the words of John Adams. As cited at the start of chapter II:

America is a great, unwieldy Body. Its Progress must be slow. It is like a large Fleet sailing under Convoy. The fleetest Sailors must wait for the dullest and slowest.

And as you can imagine, our Captain plays a prominent role in our story. So, let's be clear regarding the definition of our Captain. Our Captain is not a person. Our Captain is the assembled collection of those we have entrusted with our government, and you will find this point frequently made.

(6) Due to the overwhelming importance of our 2nd President, John Adams, the younger President Adams, J. Quincy Adams, who is also often considered to be within the Top 20, has been neglected. All mentions of President Adams herein refer to the elder, John Adams.

(7) Capitalization rules have been liberalized to elevate certain words and ideas to their proper places. This is explained in chapter XVII, *Our Metaphysics*:

The fact is, these notions are not merely words. They are a fundamental part of our tangled reality – each is among the enduring characters within the passing stories of our lives, and we must know them.

(8) Some readers may conclude that this work was written during the last couple of years, but such is not the case. The work was largely completed

by 2015. It has been published in 2024 only because of the compelling nature of this day.

I hope that you find THOUGHT CHOICE POWER, borne of and supported by the words of our historical Top 20 Presidents and a few other pillars of Western philosophy, to be thought-provoking and as worthy of your time as the subject itself.

- i am Plebeius

THOUGHT
CHOICE
POWER

Charting the Course of Liberty in Modern Society

Introduction

In Respect to Leadership

Progress occurs when courageous, skillful leaders seize the opportunity to change things for the better.[1]

– Harry S. Truman

History proves humanity's voyage through Time to be neither smooth nor uncomplicated.

The Record also shows us that, to better cope, people have used various attachments of commonality – purposed bindings apt to coalesce into communities, states, and nations. These attachments, while coupled, harness the power in numbers – they effectually combine the forever shifting strengths, weaknesses, fears, desires, beliefs, experiences, and expectations of people into rather peculiar bodies, into systems that sooner or later require competent administration and skilled management. Such is the essence of civilization – of the societal ties that bind us – and, despite the opposite convictions of some, each society requires leadership.

As President Truman knew, progress depends on functional leadership. It shapes the trajectory and coherence of any civilization, guiding people through challenges, changes, and advancements in their collective journey.

Leaders of peoples, often rulers of one kind or another, are as varied as those led and tend to reflect some underlying disposition of the particular social order in which he or she was raised. But regardless of type or pedigree, or the fact that leadership graduates in degrees of difficulty as a society grows larger or more diverse, all leaders are inevitably judged during their day and later alike by their ability to chart a course and then steer their society. Hence, the skills common to all leadership are those of assessment, analysis, resolve, communication, supervision, and inspiration, not to mention a healthy respect for institutional continuity.

And irrespective of the path taken or the magnitude and multiplicity of a people, it is nearly always true that the most effective leaders possess an aptitude for the maneuver – a capability to successfully negotiate moments of material jeopardy and an aspiration to rightly answer the many questions destined to influence days still over the horizon.

Unfortunately, despite the condition of any given society or its level of satisfaction related to its leadership – selected or not – the marking of Time upon The Record never ceases, and when leadership is absent, or largely deficient, most of that society is subjected to forces far outside their command. When leadership is not up to the task, the people's attachments begin to break down, and the people themselves are eventually left to their own devices. The people inevitably become high and dry Plebeians compelled to hang about the never-ending ways of the Patricians – they are left to stand and await the conclusion of their day while anchored to its wheel tracks by the heavy weight of trepidation.

We the People are, of course, different, for We have not a ruler nor chariots.

Yet, distinct as We so wish to consider ourselves, when caught up in a fog of inadequate leadership – when the moment looks to be developed beyond our capacity to manage, and it seems as if We are not in control of our lives – easy does it become to point our fingers and to assign blame for our troubles while, at the same time, the various political animals work to foment distrust and dissent in their effort to attain, solidify, or regain their power as calculated in their playbooks of politics.

It is sad to say, but We, the People, have been far too frequently inclined to stand still[ii] – to overlook the

---

ii The phrase "*In periods where there is no leadership, society stands still*" is often attributed to Harry Truman but lacks definitive source attribution. While this quote aligns with Truman's views on leadership, it remains undocumented in his official records. The full quote commonly cited, parts of which are attributable, is: "*Men make history and not the other way around. In periods where there is no leadership, society stands still. Progress occurs when courageous, skillful leaders seize the opportunity to change things for the better.*" Our usage of "stand still" aligns with the spirit of Truman's believed perspective, thus this tip of the cap acknowledgement.

breadth of our responsibilities and the extent of our collective might – to choose instead to lay blame at the feet of others and to divide ourselves along the familiar fault lines of factional frenzy, thereby furthering our distress as well as the Dysfunction of the day...

PART ONE

THOUGHT

If men were angels, no government would be necessary. If angels were to govern men, neither external nor internal controls on government would be necessary. In framing a government which is to be administered by men over men, the great difficulty lies in this: you must first enable the government to control the governed; and in the next place oblige it to control itself.[iii]

– James Madison

---

iii "The Federalist No. 51, [6 February 1788]," *Founders Online*, National Archives, https://founders.archives.gov/documents/Hamilton/01-04-02-0199. [Original source: *The Papers of Alexander Hamilton*, vol. 4, *January 1787–May 1788*, ed. Harold C. Syrett. New York: Columbia University Press, 1962, pp. 497–502.]

I

The Helm

The bulk of the people are for democracy, and if they are well inform'd the ruin of such enterprizes [wayward government] will infallibly follow.[2]

— James Monroe

Throughout history, the condition of humanity has waxed and waned with the tide of the Times – pitching and rolling and yawing, occasionally finding repose amid the events of the day. This We understand.

So, too, do We understand the efforts of the individual to be relevant amid the considerations and follies of those situated at the helm. Thus, We should by now be able to recognize when leadership has lost its way. We ought to understand why We, the People, must be forever prepared to remedy all wayward uses of our collective trust along with the repercussions thereof. This is particularly important within the context of our shared Federal Government, our utmost essential structure.

Truth is – If the ideals borne of our Forefathers' rebellion and reared by their heirs are to endure, then We of the eternally present day must always be ready and willing to correct our course. The simple fact that We are imperfect does not relieve us of our choices. Therefore, We must take stock of this day – one wherein Privilege has shed its thin veil – a moment in Time where it is absurdly difficult for a sincere and knowledgeable person to declare our structures of governance and economy fit, functioning as was intended by those generations to which We owe our existence.

Easy it is to see that We have long been entrusting our government to individuals exhibiting little regard for the progress of our condition. Their policies, past and present, have combined to limit our economic opportunities and the positive outcomes contained therein. We have erred. We have submitted as our assembled Captain has seen to it that our structure of governance has come to be occupied by the masters of our economy, so much so that it is reasonable for an outsider to ask if the People still hold a genuine link to their vessels.

Time it is for us to awaken, to be neither timid nor misunderstood as We say that We cannot – We the People will not – allow those delegated the controls of our Nation to squander our vessels of Liberty. We need all come to be familiar with these rather blunt words of President Thomas Jefferson:

...what country can preserve its liberties if their rulers are not warned from time to time that their people preserve the spirit of resistance?[3]

To be clear, our expectations of our Captain have always been sincere – We do not wish our government to be our provider, nor do We want our government to be our master. We expect those We entrust to work for our benefit as it is balanced against the benefit of our fellow citizens regardless of their rank. We of the crew expect those at the helm to ensure a safe and sustained environment teeming with Opportunity, perpetually fortifying in length, width, and durability the corridors in which We can improve upon our individual stations if We so diligently choose. Our labors and the consequences thereof should never be discounted by the impulses of a relative few.

We have become all too aware of how one's initial station in life is too often predictive of life's outcome. We have had enough of unsteady paths and unfavorable odds due to our Captain being content with the destiny of those in the swelling bowels of our ships. We are tired of standing still while those We entrust act obliged to the monied and their desires for control.

This Nation is ours too, and the moment has come for those We choose "to stand in [our] places" to ensure that our government effectively offsets the weights of both unadulterated favors and combinations of men and women attempting to amass influences far more significant than that allowed by any equitable law of proportionality. High time it is for our Captain to become reacquainted with the specific powers and authorities granted to it, enumerated in Article I, Section 8 of our Constitution. In this is what We expect:

> *The Congress shall have Power (1) To lay and collect Taxes, Duties, Imposts and Excises, to pay the Debts and provide for the common Defence and general Welfare of the United States...; (2) To borrow Money on the credit of the United States; (3) To regulate Commerce with foreign Nations, and among the several States, and with the Indian Tribes; (4) To establish a uniform Rule of Naturalization...; (5) To coin Money, regulate the Value thereof, and of foreign Coin...; (6) To promote the Progress of Science and useful Arts...; (7) To declare War...; and (8) To make all Laws which shall be necessary and proper for carrying into Execution the foregoing Powers vested by this Constitution...*[4]

This day, let us plainly state that it is not our objective to either subvert our Constitution or supplant our Free Enterprise structure. We believe that our Nation can be born again without a dramatic upheaval and that the foresight of our Founders provides us with the mechanisms required to correct the negligent gyrations of those We have mistakenly entrusted with the helm. But, be not mistaken – our cause is neither light nor transient – a mutiny is brewing outside the Captain's tower.

II

A Large Fleet

America is a great, unwieldy Body. Its Progress must be slow. It is like a large Fleet sailing under Convoy. The fleetest Sailors must wait for the dullest and slowest.[5]

– John Adams

Given the unrelenting and torrential nature of information this day, our steady diet of consequential bits and bytes has left us longing for the truth. Distracted, confused, concerned, angry, somewhat fearful, and bloated with cynical wonder, our lives are increasingly complicated. Nonetheless, as We scurry about within the confines of our modern reality – laden with the chores of having to filter and synthesize countless loads of reports, broadcasts, gossip, hearsay, editorial, spin, rumor, and lies – We now realize that the events of our day tend to unfold at breakneck speeds in concert with unprecedented momentums, and We are fully aware of the recurring characteristic of our difficulties.

Moreover, it has become easy to see that our institutional ballasts of government are incapable of effectively dealing with almost any issue of real significance. We need not catalog specifics, from mundane to monumental – some upon us, others festering. There are many. Our problems have graduated beyond a list of succinct grievances. Aye, the root of our distress is the inability of lawmakers and their cronies at the federal level to recognize and effectively act upon the vast interconnectivity of our seemingly singular issues.

Fiscal policy, monetary policy, defense, societal deals, energy, commerce, foreign entanglements, the environment, terrorism, trade, immigration, labor, justice, education, health care, etc. Are We to believe that our Captain can manage each of these matters in relative isolation? Are We really to accept the proposition that the subsets of each political heading – the dirty work of democratic governance – can be successfully dealt with aside from the overarching umbrella that is our economy? To be sure, as our political class struggles in their infantile ways, the waters of our world roil progressively out of our control.

Fact is, We the People live and work within the most compounded of realms, the most confounding seen to date, and it should be clear to all of us that – unless We are to flirt with collapsing under our weight – We must be up to the task of protecting the structural integrity of our System. We must acknowledge that We jeopardize our grasp upon our standards when We duck our essential responsibilities of Independence, particularly when We fail to appreciate the meanings and the purposes of the words Government and Economy.

So it is that We all need to understand our conflated reality – our dual structures of Government and Economy – the respective agents of union and work which combine in one way or another to form the whole of any System.

We must know these definitions: (1) Government is the arrangement of political institutions, laws, and customs through which the function of governing is carried out, and (2) Economy is nothing less than the productive management of the resources of a group of people, be that group a household or a community or a state or a nation. How can We hold our Captain to account if We do not know the most essential of definitions adhered to our System?

Also, We must recognize our day for what it is – a moment in which the inherent fragility of the ideals of our Forefathers, and the Rights of Equality later earned by way of the many high sacrifices made in confronting our hypocrisies, shall not survive the tests of Time if We, the People, either resign our posts or remain ambivalent towards our need to entrust those most capable of nimble and justly principled leadership to our helm. Our work and mission are too vital for us to choose the unqualified.

We have each been transformed into an elemental part of a dynamic and extraordinarily complex Political

Economy, afloat within a sea of uncertainty. We have collectively become a titanic civilization requiring sensible oversight and competent guidance, and just as never do the waters stand still for long, neither does our need for good decisions.

Hence, if We are to progress, We can ill afford to be either stricken by an increasing onslaught of information or ignorant about the fundamentals of our System, and We should often refresh our senses with these words bequeathed to us by President James Madison:

> *In the Constitution, the great ends of government were particularly enumerated; but all the means were not, nor could they all be, pointed out, without making the Constitution a complete code of laws: some discretionary power, and reasonable latitude, must be left to the judgment of the legislature.*[6]

Under the power of sail, We are not, and thus our paradox: Try as We might to still order our lives in a linear fashion, back and forth in simplistic balance, going to work and then returning to the relative solace of our quarters and our private endeavors while the Captain continues to carry out the larger decisions of our advancement, the equation of life these days has come to be increasingly highlighted by relationships entwined and connections layered, a reality folded many times over with threads all through. This is why our intrinsic desire to live an uncomplicated life is challenged.

The simple person be damned if our System, our fleet, cannot survive the challenges of this complex world.

III

Heading

It should be the highest ambition of every American to extend his views beyond himself, and to bear in mind that his conduct will not only affect himself, his country, and his immediate posterity; but that its influence may be co-extensive with the world, and stamp political happiness or misery on ages yet unborn.[7]

– George Washington

As sure as history is habitually distorted, no person can see forward into the continuum of Time. No one can say with certainty what tomorrow will bring, and there exists not a soul amongst us with a perfect view beyond that of which the horizon has to offer. Yet, even if only in general terms, we can chart our course and foresee to where We are headed. We can correlate where We have been with the overall direction of this drifted day that is.

We have the ability – if honest with ourselves – to avoid the familiar storm fast approaching off the starboard beam.

Have We not been degrading our Democracy, defacing our Republic, and denigrating our livelihoods? Have We not supported both a political environment wherein the monied rule and a manner of governing whereby little of significance can be accomplished unless a single Faction has near complete control? Have We not fostered an Economy wherein the incomes of our ballyhooed middle class lay as flat as do the plans so neatly unfurled inside the properties of the well-constructed cadre of global elite?

Indeed, We can see the way in which We are headed. Still, to do so, We must reflect – however annoying to some – upon the fact that in 1775 many of the thirteen soon-to-be States asked John Adams for his counsel regarding the creation of their governments and constitutions. Adams, widely considered by his contemporaries their foremost theoretical authority on governmental structures and later to be our 2nd President, responded with his seminal work, *Thoughts on Government*. It is inside the bindings of his esteemed blueprint, which went on to provide much of the structure for our Federal Government, where Adams expressed the following:

> *We ought to consider, what is the end of government, before we determine which is the best*

form. Upon this point all speculative politicians will agree, that the happiness of society is the end of government, as all Divines and moral Philosophers will agree that the happiness of the individual is the end of man. From this principle it will follow, that the form of government, which communicates ease, comfort, security, or in one word happiness to the greatest number of persons, and in the greatest degree, is the best.[8]

Thusly begged is a question: Would anyone amongst us like to step forward under cover of open debate and argue against "ease, comfort, security, or, in one word, happiness" – the conjoined cravings of humankind – as being the very reason why We have our Government as constituted? To be sure, any a taker would have little respect for the words "If men were angels…", and President Adams would have deemed them cast from the absurd – foolish for discounting the wisdom within "you must first enable the government to control the governed; and in the next place oblige it to control itself."

And can We not agree that President Adams would find the years since his passing filled with corroborating evidence – awash with illustrations of people laboring under the weight of oppressive governments? Cannot We agree that Adams, while he would this day find Security amply impressed upon the psyche of his countrymen, would be perplexed as to how We managed to warp the words Ease and Comfort as he aligned them alongside "happiness to the greatest number of persons, and in the greatest degree"?

Yes, there will always be those forever yearning to place the twisted tenets of their own brand of capitalism – and freedom – above the wisdom of President Adams, so let us be clear when We say that as sure as some are to deride our words so too have they long scoffed, privately as a rule, at the more significant implications sewn within these not so trivial words attributed to our 3rd President, Thomas Jefferson:

> *We hold these truths to be self-evident, that all men are created equal, that they are endowed by their Creator with certain unalienable Rights, that among these are Life, Liberty and the pursuit of Happiness.*[9]

Our Government was designed to justly advance an environment conducive to the expansion of "happiness to the greatest number of persons, and in the greatest degree" – to promote each person's respective Pursuit of Ease and Comfort within the Security of a safe and sound society – to allow each of us to live our Life and exercise our Liberty in the name of our individual Happiness as lawfully restrained by the common boundaries which We share with our fellow citizens. Regrettably, We have been willing to turn from this primary intent – instead, entrusting our Government to individuals determined to detach our political affairs from the measurable effects of our economic policies.

We have allowed ourselves to be distracted and divided by drivel, always eager to emphasize our private differences over our public commonalities. And as We struggle to recognize the common threads of our existence, our System is being pulled apart – distorted to the extent that Political Economy has been, in fact, scrubbed from our thoughts.

In how many ways do We need to say it?

As a people, We have impaired our interests and those of our descendants. We have watched as our System has been placed on a heading whereby the ideals of our Forefathers steadily succumb to the wanton desires of a fortunate few, from near and far alike. We have even tolerated the mounting pressures for ever quicker salutes as our Government has failed to protect us within our intended framework of justice. We have been compliant, having allowed the entrusted to fixate on their electoral gains instead of economic policies that foster sustainable, long-term, economic growth. Not to mention the fact that our Captain has done nothing, quite literally, to address the ever-widening gap in our distribution of wealth. And now our moment is upon us.

Hence, if our bearings are to be restored, then We need here and now – in uncomplicated terms – enunciate what we expect of our Political Economy…

So that we may go about a just Pursuit of our Ease and Comfort, let it be known that We expect to be shielded within the context of our working lives. Our most basic of wants connected to our Political Economy is for our Government to reasonably function as a conduit and catalyst within our shared sphere of commerce. After all, is this not our intended heading – a shared System beyond that of Security wherein our structures of Government and Economy operate on behalf of the People?

If still confused as to our hopes surrounding "ease, comfort, security, or, in one word, happiness," knowing that some shall resist and even more shall lag, then the following words spoken by President Theodore Roosevelt should provide enough understanding as to what We expect of our Political Economy:

> *Far and away the best prize that life offers is the chance to work hard at work worth doing; and this is a prize open to every man*[10]

We deem these words of President Roosevelt to be the quintessential explanation of our American Dream. Why? Because "[working] hard at work worth doing" should generate tangible results, "[working] hard at work worth doing" should afford some modest degree of Ease of Life, "[working] hard at work worth doing" should result in a relative measure of Comfort, and "[working] hard at work worth doing" should illuminate many a Corridor of Opportunity.

Enough is enough. We can no longer afford to allow "work worth doing" to be equated with work of any kind, work that will likely never lead to a better Opportunity for either this generation or the next, work for the sake of work irrespective of the components of Life that relate to Happiness, and We certainly cannot afford to continue with our current ways of work while allowing ourselves to be alienated politically.

We can no longer afford – recognizing what We can see today – to underestimate the likelihood that our present heading is leading us into very troubled waters, for with each sunrise of apathy does a tempest grow as per these words of President Franklin D. Roosevelt:

> *The first truth is that the liberty of a democracy is not safe if the people tolerate the growth of private power to a point where it becomes stronger than their democratic state itself. That, in its essence, is fascism – ownership of government by an individual, by a group, or by any other controlling private power.*[11]

Is it not safe to say that each President Roosevelt, as well as Presidents Jefferson, Adams, and Washington, would this day be astounded by "the growth of private power" and our penchant to sell it as anything but? Would they not agree with the sentiment of many that We have nonchalantly arranged a state wherein the most basic tenets used to hold together the foundation of our Representative Democracy are ignored? Aye, they would question why we have obediently carved ourselves into distinctly different bodies with little in common save for an ability to feed the flames of Faction. They would warn us of the woe coming our way if We continue to be indifferent towards "the ownership of government by an individual, by a group."

Fact is, our propensity to disregard the more perilous inclinations of mankind is sure to shadow exaggerated levels of satisfaction with our Political Economy, and most any of our finest Presidents would warn us that if We do not change course We will eventually be confronted by some variant form of tyranny – they would tell us that We will be faced in a while if not much sooner with a technologically equipped tyrant of our own making.

Moreover, The Record tells us that it matters not if one is to cope with a despot on the left or a despot on the right, as each is undoubtedly related in ways and intent.

We must be honest with ourselves!

We are constructing an entity of historical Dysfunction. We are rearing a multi-headed monolithic monarchy fated to dictate our lives as it sees fit. In reasonably practical terms, We the People are preparing our way of Life to be scuttled, and lest our Nation perish as our possession, We need to see that our course does change.

This is our cause – this is our calling. This is our revolution.

IV

Negligence

The people of these United States are the rightful masters of both congresses and courts, not to over-throw the Constitution, but to over-throw the men who pervert that Constitution.[12]

– Abraham Lincoln

What is Negligence? In legal terms, Negligence is behavior deemed to be outside the bounds of reasonable conduct as both (a) related to the protection of others against unjust injury or risk thereof and (b) compared to the likely choices of a typically sensible individual placed in a similar situation. It should go without having to be said that those We entrust ought to understand the definition of Negligence along with its standing within our System – which is to say that the choices made by those We entrust, as well as their appointees, should always reflect a commitment to Care and Prudence within our structures of Government and Economy.

Unfortunately, aside from being a vast museum, far too many of us now see Washington, D.C., as little more than the principal playground on which those possessing a dramatically elevated need for say pursue their partisan objectives – the coordinate around which an inexhaustible war of words and dirty deeds serves to direct and divide our mass into more manageable cliques within a grand framework of self-serving Faction. As to this there should be little doubt, nor should there be much doubt as to why We have grown tired of our supposed leaders pursuing their agendas without proper considerations being afforded the majority of us.

It is so very disheartening, the realization that the bulk of the entrusted have long been conducting themselves in such a manner so as to (1) subordinate our endeavors and minimize our prospects, (2) encourage fantastical schemes of speculation, (3) raid our Treasury, (4) corrupt our currency, and (5) laden future generations with astonishing levels of debt, all while (6) inviting quandary and consternation in foreign lands. In addition, while wallowing in the swill of their Dysfunction, Congress has managed to (7) consistently weaken itself relative to the powers of the presidency and (8) bear out a politicized Supreme Court of debatable intent, thereby diminishing the voice of the People and assaulting the safeguards designed to prevent usurpation.

No, our Captain has not been demonstrably concerned with our precepts of Care and Prudence.

And so it is that We, "the rightful masters", must rectify the oh-so proudly derived impediments to our progress, including the heavy weight of inaction. Still, We ought not to suppose that We too are not without considerable blame. If true to our cause We must also indict ourselves, as We have negligently assumed our Republic capable of effectively navigating the seas of circumstance upon which humanity sails while We, in effect, neglect our duties – not the least of which are those of thoughtful election and the need to mine that which is to be learned from yesteryear.

We have become content with playing the lead in a farcical conflict of Either-Or, seemingly happy with our roles of proxy and choosing sides as if We were at some great sporting event, more than willing to act as if our Declaration of Independence and or our Constitution orders us to pledge our allegiances to political parties. We have all but deserted our posts of responsibility.

Truth is – We have divided ourselves to the point that the eponym of our Capital City, if he could see us today, would be altogether embarrassed with having his good name attached to it. How is it that We have come to disregard the wisdom of our 1st and arguably finest President, especially his words of warning related to Faction, the most natural of the many threats to our chosen arrangement of Government?

We should be ashamed, and We ought not to continue flouting this wise counsel within President

Washington's 1796 Farewell Address, so aptly presented to his "Friends and Fellow-Citizens":

> *All obstructions to the execution of the laws, all combinations and associations, under whatever plausible character, with the real design to direct, control, counteract, or awe the regular deliberation and action of the constituted authorities, are destructive of this fundamental principle, and of fatal tendency. They serve to organize faction, to give it an artificial and extraordinary force; to put, in the place of the delegated will of the nation the will of a party, often a small but artful and enterprising minority of the community; and, according to the alternate triumphs of different parties, to make the public administration the mirror of the ill-concerted and incongruous projects of faction, rather than the organ of consistent and wholesome plans digested by common counsels and modified by mutual interest.*[13]

Are We not this day functionally ignorant regarding the parting declaration of President Washington? Are We, the People, no longer capable of comprehending George Washington's place within The Record, and are his words "of fatal tendency" not clear, concise and worthy of our attention? What exactly is there not to understand regarding "all obstructions to the execution of the laws...with the real design to direct, control, counteract, or awe the regular deliberation and action of the constituted authorities"? Have We become oblivious to human nature, incapable of comprehending the natural rapport between the base forces of Faction and a negligent Captain? Just how is it that We have come to be so apathetic about the perils of Faction? These are grave questions.

Also, there exists not a single good excuse for us to be unaware of the fact that President Washington himself bore witness to the first bona fide factional divide amongst our Founders and that he alerted us as to the hazards capable of eroding even the commonalities of revolutionary compatriots.

George Washington watched the unraveling of the bond between Founding Fathers John Adams and Thomas Jefferson, our 2nd and 3rd Presidents, each possessing good intentions and intellects ranking them amongst the absolute finest philosophical minds in American history. Moreover, the saga of Adams and Jefferson is our own and speaks to the risks woven within our scheme of Faction.

This is to say that with but a bit of study some of us might be inclined to conclude that our reality today was birthed by the contentious debate leading up to the 1787 ratification of the Constitution itself – the structural keel on top of which our societal arrangements are built – with the so-called Federalists in support and the so-called Anti-Federalists in opposition. Likewise, with but a bit of study, We might see that it was during President Washington's first term in office when the Federalists, including then Vice President Adams, formally became the Federalist Party (led by Secretary of the Treasury Alexander Hamilton), while the greater part of the Anti-Federalists plus a few others, most notably James Madison, more or less morphed to become the Democrat-Republican Party (rather un-admittedly led by then Secretary of State Jefferson). With but a bit of study, some might even conclude that our current Dysfunction is related to the evolved fallout from Adams versus Jefferson. However, such an argument would be hard-pressed to assume equally good intentions from the different players today.

Furthermore, no good do We do ourselves when We know not that upon the election of 1796 the Federalist Adams succeeded Washington as President, and since the law of the day dictated that the candidate receiving the second highest number of votes serve as Vice President, the Anti-Federalist Jefferson was elected V.P. in opposition. No good do We do ourselves when We ignore the fact that the election of 1800 saw Vice President Jefferson defeat President Adams, leaving their one-time close relationship so tattered that Adams did not bother attending the swearing into office of his compatriot.

And no good do We do ourselves when We overlook the crescendo of our early factional melodrama – the 1804 death of Alexander Hamilton, an extraordinarily influential Founding Father killed in a dual consequential to callous words of politics by none other than President Jefferson's sitting Vice President, Aaron Burr.

Regardless of whether We wish to know or even acknowledge it, our System has always been messy. And now – some ten generations removed from our founding – Negligence reigns.

We can no longer afford to discount these next words within Washington's Farewell Address:

> *However combinations or associations of the above description may now and then answer popular ends, they are likely, in the course of time and things, to become potent engines, by which cunning, ambitious, and unprincipled men will be enabled to subvert the power of the people and to usurp for themselves the reins of government, destroying afterwards the very engines which have lifted them to unjust dominion.*[14]

Let us thusly and without reservation acknowledge that President Washington's warning rings not hollow this day, that his words constitute a timeless reminder of the difficulties of binding together the natural differences of opinions and conclusions sure to reside within the borders of any Democracy.

Let us concede that our collected body of political want, our Government, with its many hands upon the controls of our System, cannot be expected to cast off its unhealthy behaviors and function as intended if We the People are insistent upon turning our backs in hope – resigned to allowing "combinations and associations under whatever plausible character" to take over and direct the workings of our Economy, and by natural extension the gears of our individual lives, in an egocentric or otherwise dysfunctional manner.

Let us admit that We cannot ensure the stability of our System if We remain ambivalent regarding our historical Dysfunction and agreeable to the intentions of a determined few – those who undoubtedly consider "consistent and wholesome plans digested by common counsels and modified by mutual interest" to be but charming and far too complex for the abilities of our imaginations.

Fact is, with so many conclusions to be drawn by such a substantial number of people – bad intentions aside – if We are to have a fighting chance at coalescing our wants and our opinions in the name of self-governance, then a majority of us must be both committed to studying the lessons of the past and quick to encourage every virtuous opposition to Faction. In other words, if We as a Nation still possess a want to rely upon our Constitution and "the execution of [its] laws" as the platform upon which our society is to rise above the challenges of an unstable world, if goodness yet remains within us, then We must also have the desire to utilize President Washington's tack as he here plotted:

> *We ought not to look back, unless it is to derive*
> *useful lessons from past errors – & for the*
> *purpose of profiting by dear bought experience*

– To enveigh against things that are past &
irremediable, is unpleasing – but to steer clear
of the shelves & rocks we have struck upon, is the
part of wisdom – equally incumbent on political,
as other men, who have their own little bark; or
that of others to navigate through the intricate
paths of life, or the trackless ocean to the haven
of secury & rest.[15]

Collectively and individually alike, We must admonish all obstinate disregard for the wisdom within The Record, and rebuke all irresponsible ways of political parties. We must acknowledge that our Nation cannot reliably advance within the enlightened construct of our Constitution if We remain compliantly numb, accepting of a Government incapable of creating and or executing virtuous decisions because neither the Captain nor the crew can escape the constraints of Faction.

Lest We, the People, are to rely upon unadulterated luck, We must agree that choices borne of either Ignorance or carelessness will surely hinder our ability to correct our course as needed, for in our case, such choices are forms of Negligence and never shall either be blissful.

Alas – even if, while acknowledging the not-so-perfect drama that is our historical stage, We confess to our own failings, and even if We concede that We do ourselves no good when We accept either conscious disregard or Ignorance as a sturdy foundation for our ability to choose wisely – it is practically impossible to shake the sense that the bulk of the entrusted seem dedicated to casually ignoring our Happiness. And with this now in full view, We the People, alarmed by those outwardly inclined to deep-six our Constitution, must question our readiness to insist upon reasonably constructed societal rules duly enforced and judiciously strengthened by those whom We send into our service.

Are you ready to ensure that our society rightly values the precepts of Care and Prudence, and do you agree that We the People are indeed "the rightful masters"? Your response decides whether you align with Care and Prudence and good Government, or oppressive Negligence.

Which side are YOU on?

V

Duty

The aim of every political constitution is, or ought to be, first to obtain for rulers men who possess most wisdom to discern, and most virtue to pursue, the common good of the society; and in the next place, to take the most effectual precautions for keeping them virtuous whilst they continue to hold their public trust.[16]

– James Madison

Assuming We the People are interested in some standard of Care and Prudence within our System and that We appreciate our shared role therein, We need to calibrate our thinking to what President Madison called "the aim of every political constitution." Over and above our basic need for Discernment, We must develop a functional understanding of a person's "virtue to pursue" in relation to that same person's likely choices concerning "the common good of the society".

Lest We are a ship of fools, unable or unwilling to acknowledge our responsibilities and impediments, We must be able to enunciate the inverse nature of the relationship between Virtue and Negligence. We must ensure that those We entrust – our assembled Captain – possess enough Virtue to keep Negligence at bay.

This ought to be easy. If We are willing to hoist our banners of Care and Prudence high, then enforcing Madison's requisites of "most wisdom to discern, and most virtue to pursue" should come quickly.

And let us not underestimate the words "keeping them virtuous". Fact is, We will sometimes stumble when choosing those that should possess the "most wisdom to discern" – with our blunders nearly sure to test our stability – but failing to "[keep] them virtuous" is an entirely different matter, for such failures are guaranteed to create a degree of Negligence destined to amplify the Dysfunction already rippling throughout our System.

Besides, We the People should by now realize that there will always be those looking to degrade the Virtue of others. We should be willing to protect the stability of our structures per Madison's instruction to "[keep] them virtuous".

Hardly any effort should it take for us to identify the two prime suspects in the assault on our System's Virtue, three if the 24-hour entertainment news cycle is counted.

First is the amount of money now strewn throughout our political process, namely cash used to manipulate campaigns and persuade officials, with every dollar intended to pervert those We have entrusted and our structures. Second are the "red meat" forces of Party Politics, the incessant nonsense that promotes a process wherein the candidate furthest removed from the ever-shifting political center is regularly rewarded. Lastly, though not a formal element of our structures, the abovementioned and underestimated third element does indeed constitute a powerful tool even in and of itself.

Seeing as our assailants undoubtedly have at least one trait in common, We would serve ourselves well by requiring those We entrust, and their appointees, to adorn their office walls with these words of President Adams:

I have always been convinced that abuse of Words, has been the great instrument of Sophistry and Chicanery – of party, faction and Division in Society[17]

We are careless when ignoring Adams' "abuse of Words", so let us here work backward, surveying our third factor first.

Truth is – The principal reality of the 24-hour information cycle is one of Money and influence, not enlightenment, and as We have gone about giving applause aplenty to concerted affairs of persuasion contorted around self-styled experts of intended purpose and secondhand political players and wannabes and well-worded reporters of not so well-hidden agendas and bigheaded pundits, We have lost sight of the facts that each is too often devoid of accountability and more than a few are paid a King's ransom for their ability to keep or sway our attention. Our information has become as corrupt as the political game itself.

We must be realistic regarding the relationship between the monied, the media, and our politicians. We need to realize that the choreographed moments of revenue-generating corporate shenanigans that We are ceaselessly fed, along with the growing multitude of others, serve to distort the fields upon which our depraved players of politics perform their factional assignments.

If We would but give proper consideration to the impact of Time upon the means, then We might realize that these words of President Washington are even more relevant today:

> *If the government and the officers of it are to be the constant theme for newspaper abuse, and this too without condescending to investigate the motives or the facts, it will be impossible, I conceive, for any [person] living to manage the helm or to keep the machine together.*[18]

"Red or Blue? Choose NOW" goes the perpetual drumbeat because the other We are told is not worthy of, altogether incapable of, and or surreptitiously not in favor of furthering our best interests, much less the ephemeral contentment of Happiness. Make no mistake, We have submitted ourselves to the spellbinding antics of bipolar Party Politics while hardly pausing to ponder this primary predicament now woven within our System – a quandary so woefully glossed over inside our classrooms that We weaken ourselves each passing day.

Moreover, We cannot shine too bright a light upon our own Negligence, as We have ensured that there exist great difficulties for any autonomous voice to be objectively heard. Quite many of us, owing to either disgust or laziness, do not participate; scores of us have tilted toward one Party owing to a disdain for a few elements, if not just one or two of the other; more than a few of us have been inclined to vote straight party-line; and if We shall be honest with ourselves, far less than a few of us are actually up to our democratic responsibility of voting since a genuine preparedness would entail an ability to be neither influenced by warped words of spin and advertisement nor overwhelmed by the sheer volume of information and disinformation that is heaved upon us.

We have not exhibited much Care and Prudence nor demanded it from those We have entrusted.

We have herded ourselves towards one sideline or the other – following the stench of rotting tongues while willfully oblivious to the constant swapping of influence for Money – yet We wonder why it now feels as if the majority of the entrusted view our ability to progress as little more than a quaint if not an annoying concept relegated to derivative status, contingent upon the selfish desires of those having monetized our System. We have proven ourselves unconcerned with Virtue, Dysfunction has become the norm, and We have thusly arrived at this place of desperate need for Reasonable Persons to step forward and lead.

Little reason is there for any of us to be befuddled. Money in and of itself is relatively harmless, irrespective of where it resides. However, the prime perversion related to Money is still precisely as has been delineated many a year past. How little has changed in the minds of humanity since this observation of President Washington:

Few men have virtue to withstand the highest bidder.[19]

Aye, the lineages of the Monied Interests are long, and forever are they entrenched in direct opposition to the want of a people to possess a well-managed machine of just objectives. Greed, peddled sway, bribery, and cravings for dominance are nothing new to the historical stage. Virtue has always been under attack. And it is now impossible to exaggerate the perils to which We expose ourselves when We choose to ignore the significance of electing only those with enough Virtue that they might this day turn the tide against the enemies of good Government.

Hence, knowing that those with ill intent are almost sure to brand our words populist, dangerous, delusional, or paranoid, We need to highlight a candid sampling from a few of our concerned Presidents. We need to realize that President Lincoln once reminded, within the context of the State Bank of Illinois, "these capitalists generally act harmoniously, and in concert, to fleece the people"[iv]; that President Woodrow Wilson wrote, "The government, which was designed for the people, has got into the hands of bosses and their employers, the special interests. An invisible empire has been set up above the forms of democracy"[v]; President Eisenhower warned, "we must guard against the acquisition of unwarranted influence, whether sought or unsought, by the military-industrial complex"[vi]; and President Andrew Jackson added these poignant words:

The mischief springs from the power which the monied interest derives from a paper currency, which they are able to control; from the multitude

---

iv *Collected works. The Abraham Lincoln Association, Springfield, Illinois. Roy P. Basler, editor; Marion Dolores Pratt and Lloyd A. Dunlap, assistant editors.* Lincoln, Abraham, 1809-1865. New Brunswick, N.J: Rutgers University Press, 1953.

v Wilson, Woodrow. "What Is Progress?, 1913." *Teaching American History*, Ashbrook Center at Ashland University, 2021, teachingamericanhistory.org/library/document/what-is-progress/.

vi Eisenhower, Dwight D. "Military-Industrial Complex Speech, 1961." *Avalon Project*, Yale Law School, Lillian Goldman Law Library, 2008, avalon.law.yale.edu/20th_century/eisenhower001.asp.

> *of corporations, with exclusive privileges, which they have succeeded in obtaining in the different states, and which are employed altogether for their benefit; and unless you become more watchful in your states, and check this spirit of monopoly, and thirst for exclusive privileges, you will, in the end, find that the most important powers of government have been given or bartered away, and the control over your dearest has passed into the hands of these corporations.*[20]

So as not to be misunderstood, before proceeding, let us say that (a) the nature of humankind is a constant within The Record and (b) every hypothesis as first submitted shall either crumble under the weight of humanity or be further shaped by the pressures of Time until becoming a stabilizer available for use by all peoples upon this unsteady world. That is, We should not think that any a wise word makes every word or action submitted by that person to be wise or good. People are flawed, and dogmatic customs will always be difficult for us to rise above.

But while We should never believe that a single right, or even a combination of rights, can or do negate any number of wrongs, We of the present day must always be willing to add to our foundations the maxims that Time itself has forged. Disregarding right because of wrong is akin to throwing out the proverbial baby with the bath water, and doing so destines us to repeating the wrongs of the past.

So, here lay bare the entwined roots of our Dysfunction, for strangers they are not – the Monied Interests and their preferred bedfellows, the politicians.

We have not only failed to be "watchful" – We have also effectually abandoned our stations of responsibility. We have divided ourselves and lost sight of the ties that bind us as a people. We have given in to a primordial "spirit of monopoly," to Factions of citizens and aliens alike. We have placed our interests, from the whole of Fiscal to the specifics of Trade and Education and all else thereof, into the hands of a very few that "thirst for exclusive privileges". We have stood still as our Constitution, the basis of our System, has been systematically assailed, our Political Economy seized. We have neglected our responsibilities.

Now then, so that We may begin to fulfill our Duty, We need to come to appreciate the meaning of Virtue and that which is virtuous. This is no small affair.

Though We have developed a convenient tendency to reimagine words, the truth is that our ability to embrace the rationality of the Reasonable Person as a duty-bound advocate for "the common good of the society" depends on Virtue being an intended reality.

We the People need to recognize that our disregard for Duty and our acceptance of Negligence has everything to do with our misguided ideas and false characterization of the word Virtue. We need to see that Virtue is aligned with Care and Prudence as well as Life and Liberty, that it is the mortal enemy of Negligence and Dysfunction, and that it, along with Happiness, is found repeated to a level of utmost importance by our Founders. Words do matter.

More specifically, We need to realize that Virtue is more significant than some overarching self-serving degree of gratifying decency. We must understand Virtue as did our Founders, as Aristotle explained millenniums past during the epoch of Classical Greece. We have to digress in Time, briefly, because We are at heart no different than those having come before us. We are obligated to acknowledge that long before the occasion of our Independence – when the mere definition of society was worthy of profound contemplation and wise men considered questions destined to influence the formation of our Government – many an enduring truth was declared.

Abbreviated as it may be and calculated for the begging of a closer examination by all, let us peer inside the treatise on Happiness that is *Nichomachean Ethics* (as translated by W. D. Ross). At our own peril, we have ignored the timelessness of these teachings. This instruction of Aristotle is as applicable today as was the case during the years of our Founders, as well as when first written some 2,350 years ago. Below is a suitable abridgment for us to begin to see Virtue rightly correlated to our Duty:

> *...both fear and confidence and appetite and anger and pity and in general pleasure and pain may be felt both too much and too little, and in both cases not well; but to feel them at the right*

times, with reference to the right objects, towards the right people, with the right motive, and in the right way, is what is both intermediate and best, and this is characteristic of virtue. Similarly with regard to actions also there is excess, defect, and the intermediate. Now virtue is concerned with passions and actions, in which excess is a form of failure, and so is defect, while the intermediate is praised and is a form of success; and being praised and being successful are both characteristics of virtue. Therefore virtue is a kind of mean, since, as we have seen, it aims at what is intermediate.

Again, it is possible to fail in many ways (for evil belongs to the class of the unlimited, as the Pythagoreans conjectured, and good to that of the limited), while to succeed is possible only in one way (for which reason also one is easy and the other difficult; to miss the mark easy, to hit it difficult); for these reasons also, then, excess and defect are characteristic of vice, and the mean of virtue;

For men are good in but one way, but bad in many.

Virtue, then, is a state of character concerned with choice, lying in a mean, i.e. the mean relative to us, this being determined by a rational principle, and by that principle by which the man

> *of practical wisdom would determine it. Now it is a mean between two vices, that which depends on excess and that which depends on defect; and again it is a mean because the vices respectively fall short of or exceed what is right in both passions and actions, while virtue both finds and chooses that which is intermediate. Hence in respect of its substance and the definition which states its essence virtue is a mean, with regard to what is best and right an extreme.*[21]

Is it not easy for us to see that at which we are supposed to aim – the "intermediate"? Is Virtue not sufficiently clear and understandable, especially when set against our backdrop of force-fed choices cooked up by those devoted to either Defect or Excess, by corrupted propositions of Either-Or whereby neither can unlock the irons of Negligence? Can We not see the kinship between Aristotle's "man of practical wisdom" and our Reasonable Person?

Perhaps there was nothing for Pythagoras, or Aristotle, to pass down.

But let's not be facetious. Pythagoras and Aristotle left valuable legacies behind. That said, it's important to note that both of these men were significantly flawed, yet we still should be thankful for their contributions to this world.

Regardless, within the context of our System, the Defect of Care that is ignorant disregard and the Excess of Care that is a level of control requiring the hundred eyes of Argus are each a tangible form of Negligence – each is a failure of our System that contributes to our Dysfunction – as is the Defect of Prudence that is recklessness and the Excess of Prudence that is a paralyzed level of cautiousness.

And while *Ethics* does deem Defect and Excess farther apart from one another than each is from "the mean relative to us," how waning is our moment if We cannot see our festering subsystem of Faction for what it is. Our politics of Party, ever more spun about a ubiquitous authority, is a contrivance that We have managed to modify from a reasonably stable Left-Center-Right Aristotelian model into a circular form whereby the Factions, each respectively located near three o'clock and nine o'clock along the continuum, are (1) opposed on a common border by the bulk of We the Reasonable People to our True North and (2) linked by the ugly domain of despots at our oh-so silent south.

In other words, whereas Aristotle stated that "the extremes are opposed to each other and the mean," none of us should be surprised that our political gauge has become akin to a compass needle compulsively alternating between a Faction of Defect and a Faction of Excess according to the frenetic pull of the voting masses – persuaded by a small number of egotistical agents of influence and gross sums of cash and pure favor – moving either through the variation of the magnetic majority or the opposing pull of authoritarianism.

So, seeing as The Record reads like a chronicle littered with oppressors of all sorts, and too that We seem uninterested in the ageless asset of moderation – in Virtue, and Care and Prudence – far too reasonable it is for many to believe it only a matter of moments before our bearing, our needle, experiences a reversal of sorts and comes to an abrupt halt pointing in the general direction of due south, what is sure to be a very unpleasant day of reckoning.

We the People can ill afford to continue in our current ways. We cannot continue to foster a condition wherein We must choose amongst what We deem to be the lesser of evils – failing to "both [find] and [choose] that which is intermediate." We cannot continue to accept, if We are to maintain the requisite traits of our Duty, propositions of false choices and the endless games thereof that make us the pawns of the power-hungry Monied Interests and or corrupted politicians.

Negligence, Care and Prudence, Dysfunction, Happiness, Ignorance, the standard of the Reasonable Person, Discernment, and Virtue, these words, they matter.

Our Duty is quite literally our Pursuit of Virtue – it is the hammer of evenhandedness and the breastplate of the Reasonable Person – it is the acknowledgment of the "common good of the society" and our defense in the face of Ignorance – it is the unwavering advocate of Happiness, the mortal enemy of Dysfunction, the champion of Care and Prudence, and the rightful judge of Negligence.

Our Duty is a collected quest for nothing less than the metaphysical middle point between wishful hope and domination.

Time it is to embrace our Duty – to recalibrate our thinking and to stand in opposition to the extremes.

VI

Allegiance

But merchants have no country. The mere spot they stand on does not constitute so strong an attachment as that from which they draw their gains.[22]

– Thomas Jefferson

Our day is the day of those who have exhibited neither a need for the rightful definition of Economy nor respect for our notion of Nation. It is a day marked by attachments that President Jefferson could not have envisioned – by derivatives floating about in a sea of unsubstantiated money, by incredible schemes of Pyramid and Ponzi, and by those better suited for days chockfull of castles and peasants and serfs – by tiered combinations of the insatiable, each with their stuff in hand and the many of us in tow.

Our day is a day when most of us stand still per the instructions of the Monied Interests and their merchants. We have assumed our places within an orchestrated reality designed to subject us to the opaque dealings of those with their hands in, around, or anywhere near the now magical Money Supply.

Irrespective of what our Pledge of Allegiance says, We the People have been busy resurrecting lords and ladies. We are regressing – searching for feudal days and 'my liege.'

Have We not allowed a corporation to be judged the equal of men and women of voting age? Are not most of us oblivious regarding the many professed funds eager to fuel those looking to overtake everything and everyone in their conceived paths? Have We not turned a blind eye to the crushing consequences of combinations, and do We not shrug at the stashing of cash beyond our borders and gross sums of capital sitting idle? Did We not use the words "too big to fail"?

Are We not mesmerized by long unprofitable ventures that regularly have cash transfused into them merely because the monied can imagine their day of domination, and have We not proven ourselves willing to use public funds to subsidize the existence of private concerns? Have We not?

Truth is – We have managed to degrade the real value of money while depreciating the relative value of real work. We the People have even elevated speculation to a level of significance at or above that of our labors, as evidenced by our tax code. And now it is far too reasonable to conclude that We have laid waste to our American Dream on several fronts – the very idea of "work worth doing".

It is no stretch to think that We are determined to obliterate this wisdom of President Lincoln:

> *Labor is prior to, and independent of, capital. Capital is only the fruit of labor, and could never have existed if labor had not first existed. Labor is the superior of capital, and deserves much the higher consideration.*[23]

It is easy to see that in this world of hard-to-imagine too little and never ever enough – extremes gone awry within an increasingly curious depiction of freedom – most of us have shortchanged ourselves. We became altogether ambivalent – unwilling to consider the broad implications of a global investment scheme designed to coerce as many of us as possible into partaking in its bait of refined income and fashioned share prices.

We consented to our System functioning per the wants of the Monied Interests and their merchants while We set out to stress test the ties that bind us.

Aye, somewhere along our way, We allowed ourselves to be branded citizens of an order wherein We carry on either too troubled or too busy, or both, to disturb the day while those of the Monied Interests spend their time counting and cataloging the spoils of their efforts, not the least of which are cheap workers and naive consumers and small investors wanting desperately to assemble the building blocks of the next level. Not only did We lose sight of our Duty, but We also allowed the bosses to justify theirs. We became chumps, vassals of a sort – willing to buy into false promises made by false leaders via their onslaught of bad decisions and outright lies. We allowed ourselves to become the perfect cover for the Monied Interests and their merchants.

Moreover, are We not Fiscal morons?

Even if you believe deficits and debt to be irrelevant, if you think the Money Supply is truly magical, surely you must see the value of stability and confidence within the ever-complicated workings of our System. Regardless, We have dwindled our local, State, and national stockpiles of combustible materials, i.e., the revenues required to spark our collective priorities, and We have done so while our very sick sense of what it takes for a head of household to be effective and for a family to thrive – for the next generation to be raised – has worsened. We are an afflicted society.

Positions and theories can be debated to no end, but We ought not to be surprised by our growing inequality or the chaos surrounding us. It should be apparent to all that We have been making a collective Choice consistent with the designs of a grand plan – an unqualified charade of serious Thought promoting our supposed ability to thrive as a robust Nation of service providers and consumers pulled down the path to prosperity by low taxes, corporations, and the extraordinarily wealthy the world over.

Thus, understanding that gone are the days of land runs and covered wagons and settlers, and knowing history proves that our middle class and our standing amongst the peoples of this world were fortified upon a sturdy base of manufacturing, We must acknowledge the error of our ways. We must ask ourselves how it is that We failed to place a proper valuation upon this sentiment of President Washington:

A people…, who are possessed of the spirit of commerce – who see & who will pursue their advantages, may achieve almost anything.[24]

Maybe in this Age of all things blurred – of rapidly advancing technologies and concerns commingled – We lost our collective balance. Perhaps our footing became so unsteady that We lost sight of the specifics within the bigger picture. Whatever the reason, We have neglected to account for the ramifications of an organizational scheme that considers significant numbers of wanting workers and technological advancements no different than any other asset needing to be either cultured or quarried, never mind our combined "spirit of commerce".

For far too long We have willingly discounted the consequences of corporate chiefs being governed by little more than the maximization of shareholder value – an unabashed desire on the part of the monied to radically reduce costs while scaling their revenues – often acquiring and or displacing as much of a market as is possible, irrespective of the disruptive effects upon our Economy and by natural extension our lives.

Yes, disruption is the absolute quintessential bookmark of progress, and suppressing costs and expenses – including those related to payroll, benefits, and public obligations – is indeed ingrained with common sense. These are truths that We are accustomed to and accept, as do We also accept the capital-consuming nature of technology. We understand the disruptive benefits of unfettered capitalism, but unless we intend to change our System these benefits can never be allowed to trump all else. And We certainly cannot but watch as the various suits merge and acquire our competitive footings, thereby eroding the competitive nature of our Economy.

We can no longer stand still as our Government allows the mission of the monied to combine with the waves of upheaval nowadays piled atop one another. In this, there is nothing hyperbolic.

Our Government has been permitting the management of the resources belonging to the Monied Interests and their merchants to displace the productive management of the resources belonging to us – the People – and irrespective of how many times We are told to suppose ourselves Special, We have not been miraculously excused from the reality within these words spoken by President William McKinley:

> *I do not prize the word cheap. It is not a word of hope; it is not a word of comfort; it is not a word*

of cheer; it is not a word of inspiration... Why, cheap merchandise means cheap men, and cheap men mean a cheap country; and that is not the kind of Government our fathers founded[25]

How so very rich does our state become when one merely sets aside the transient "attachments" of the monied. 'Pay no mind to those advantages and comforts and things – just line up so that your more redeeming qualities can be laid bare and tried,' this is what they have been instructing us to do. This is what our definition of Exceptional has become.

Fact is, everyone and everything is subject to the allocations of Economy, and our troubles stemming from gross inequalities of income and wealth should surprise no one. People everywhere are weakened to the degree in which their paths and provisions are flattened, regardless of how often they are told to feel "exceptional". Our System is in jeopardy.

To be clear, there can be no doubt that competing and trading both individually and corporately within our Nation as well as within the family of nations wherein standards are on a comparable plane is to be expected and encouraged, as should be the diplomacy of working with those likeminded others that lag – and technology is undoubtedly the way of the future. We do not suppose our dreams can be pursued by unfairly elevating or insulating ourselves.

We are stating that our problems involve the only sensible logic for subjecting both Opportunity and

Allegiance to the more malevolent characteristics of capital. Aye, We have obediently permitted a crooked construct whereby the Monied Interests and their merchants are allowed to unashamedly chase profits at the expense of everyone and everything in their paths, including ourselves, our structures, and our surroundings. We are stating that our troubles revolve around a current twist to an ancient dilemma – the just Pursuit of the individual's own Ease and Comfort, and Security, as each is set against the motives and methods of those more powerful.

Let us, therefore, say again that our most basic want related to our Political Economy is for our Government to reasonably function as a conduit and catalyst within our shared sphere of commerce. Our intended heading is a System wherein our structures of Government and Economy operate on behalf of the People.

Let us shout 'I will not stand still' as the ideals borne of our Forefathers' rebellion and reared by their heirs are replaced by those belonging to the Monied Interests and their merchants.

Time it is for us, We the People, to rise up and fulfill our oath of Allegiance.

PART TWO

CHOICE

Our defense is in the preservation of the spirit which prizes liberty as the heritage of all men, in all lands, every where. Destroy this spirit, and you have planted the seeds of despotism around your own doors.[vii]

– Abraham Lincoln

vii Lincoln, Abraham. "Abraham Lincoln on Preserving Liberty." *Abraham Lincoln Online*, 2018 Abraham Lincoln Online, 2018, www.abrahamlincolnonline.org/lincoln/speeches/liberty.htm. September 11, 1858 Speech at Edwardsville. Source: Collected Works of Abraham Lincoln, edited by Roy P. Basler et al.

VII

A Populace

It is only when the people become ignorant and corrupt, when they degenerate into a populace, that they are incapable of exercising the sovereignty. Usurpation is then an easy attainment, and [a] usurper soon found. The people themselves become the willing instruments of their own debasement and ruin.[26]

– James Monroe

In this day wherein We, the People, have consented to be tallied amongst the masses of this world, it is too easy to think that We are choosing to divide ourselves while simultaneously attacking the essential checks and balances so deliberately designed by our Founders. It has become far too logical to wonder if We aren't willfully weakening the ballasts of our society along with the actual attachments that bind us together.

Our truth need not be cluttered – We have fallen for the selfish desires of the few, and it is now natural to ask aloud if We are not dedicated to a process of devolvement.

It would be a good idea for us to ensure that the first lesson of civics class revolves around the following ten words of President Adams:

There never was a Democracy Yet, that did not commit suicide.[27]

Is anyone surprised that the accrued consequences stemming from the poor management of our Political Economy – especially the choices made within our counterbalances of Government – have both paralyzed our politics and treacherously pulled us into a disjointed populace?

We increasingly have little in common except the proximity of the spaces We occupy. It is sad, but We have arrived at a place in Time where it is altogether rational to question our Democratic Republic, particularly that "for which it stands". Much of the evidence is inescapable…

… We appear unable to comprehend our submission to a practice of election that relishes and rewards personality over substance. We have succumbed to an inexhaustible stream of twisted statements intentionally calibrated to split us into controllable masses of slender majority. We have become all too tolerant of corrupt cliques within our government that are outwardly intent on being derelict in their Duty as a perverse means of acquiring power. And, for good measure, by our general acceptance of interlopers aiming to influence elections and or protest those residing outside their respective districts and States, We have eviscerated our republican form.

We grow ever more mob-like with each Machiavellian cycle of voting.

Know this – The Record shall find the tone of our foolishness inconsequential, the intent of our resignation irrelevant, and it will not matter how deceit developed into the standard. Regardless of cause or reason, if We continue to allow our ostensibly benign enemies of Ignorance, complacency, corruption, and the shrill of the mob to coalesce, if We continue to stand still in afflicted disbelief as the Monied Interests run amuck within their playground of polarized politics, then our ruin will come precisely as forewarned by President Monroe.

We must reset our thinking. We need once more to acquire an appreciation for the lack of ambiguity within some of President Adams' more prophetic words, namely these:

> *There is nothing which I dread so much as a division of the republic into two great parties, each arranged under its leader, and concerting measures in opposition to each other. This, in my humble apprehension, is to be dreaded as the greatest political evil under our constitution.*[28]

To those still unconcerned, as well as our Captain, do look again to President Washington's Farewell Address, specifically to his delineation of the relationship between "faction" and "despotism" and "the ruins of public liberty", as it is here where you ought to see the destination to which We the People are headed:

> *The alternate domination of one faction over another, sharpened by the spirit of revenge, natural to party dissension, which in different ages and countries has perpetrated the most horrid enormities, is itself a frightful despotism. But this leads at length to a more formal and permanent despotism. The disorders and miseries which result gradually incline the minds of men to seek security and repose in the absolute power of an individual; and sooner or later the chief of some prevailing faction, more able or more fortunate than his competitors, turns this disposition to the purposes of his own elevation, on the ruins of public liberty.*

> *Without looking forward to an extremity of this kind (which nevertheless ought not to be entirely out of sight), the common and continual mischiefs of the spirit of party are sufficient to make it the interest and duty of a wise people to discourage and restrain it.*[29]

We can ill afford to be mistaken regarding the ramifications of our willingness to participate in the various games of Either-Or, for in doing so, We are feeding a state of binary opposition – a centrifuge of increasing velocity, akin to a tempest in its intensity. Eventually, our System – our arrangement of Government and Economy – will explosively rupture the constraints of its confining structures, heralding an ugly transformation.

If We continue down our current path, in due course, We are destined to cripple our System. We will be begging for a day of reckoning – a day when our acquiescence results in the democratic invitation to a usurper, a Captain in an exceedingly singular sense.

Indeed, our epitaph will read, "the willing instruments of their own debasement and ruin."

VIII

Sovereignty

We should never dispair. Our Situation before has been unpromising and has changed for the better, so, I trust, it will again – If new Difficulties arise, we must only put forth new Exertions and proportion our Efforts to the Exigency of the Times.[30]

– George Washington

Even if they often seem harmless, Factions in and of themselves have come to represent – in the minds of the Monied Interests and those starved for more say-so – a convenient means to trump the people's authority. As to this matter, we must agree, for it is undeniable that our Nation is of our possession only to the extent that We, the People, do indeed constitute its definitive structures.

Our Armada of Liberty can only be maintained through our own purposeful actions.

Therefore, presuming We are genuinely motivated to rouse ourselves from our slumber, our essential charge is to wrestle away from the Factions and the Monied Interests the many choices that are duly ours. If We want to end what equates to a de facto presentation of our Political Economy, our System, to narcissistic blowhards and the cult of usury alike – the latter with their various offspring always in search of more coin – an agreed upon indenturing of ourselves to their latest purposes and whims, then each of us must forever strive to be independent within our shared structures of Government and Economy.

We must live as freethinkers, free from Factions and the Monied Interests.

Let us begin by firmly affixing to our mastheads this principal maxim of President Theodore Roosevelt:

the government is us – we are the government, you and I.[31]

Now, so that our many choices might be sufficiently calibrated to the aims of our ambition – since change for the sake of change is usually no change at all – at our outset, We need to refrain from rushed action. We the People need instead to direct all our attention upon the inner workings of our decision-making. In other words, prior to and distinct from acting, and with a depth equivalent to the extraordinary extent of our responsibilities, We must examine ourselves individually.

Truth is – The full spectrum of our remedial choices will only become apparent once We have passed the light that is ever present within each of us through the prism of responsibility. More specifically, if We as a collection of individuals are to reestablish our proper bearings, then We must acknowledge that the difficulties attached to our eternal Right to choose are unmercifully compounded by the complexities of the day and relative to our desire to act responsibly. And We must be honest with ourselves!

We must acknowledge the fact that within each body – singular or otherwise – there exist ongoing struggles between different measures of awareness and unawareness that directly affect our ability to choose wisely, and that even impressive levels of understanding in conjunction with many a right intention do not guarantee an ability at any given moment to synthesize that which is going on around us into a good decision as judged by Time. This is indisputable because We are not perfect.

Moreover, We must be willing to acknowledge that (a) our "Exigency of the Times" is a set of quandaries brought about by a deterioration of our rational behaviors, and (b) Ignorance is defined as a state of unknowing naturally at odds with an adept ability to choose. If We are unwilling to acknowledge both of these facts, then it will be nearly impossible for us to understand that our capabilities related to our Free Will, and therefore our ability to conquer our problems successfully, is predicated upon an unwavering desire to learn from and then build atop wisdom borne in Time past.

Hereof is the essence of progress, of "new Exertions" – of one's desire to continue to make headway.

Now then, as We advance, it is incumbent upon us to understand that our Nation was neither formulated by some great chance nor miraculously coagulated around the belief that sovereign men could rule themselves by way of democratically elected representatives separated into multiple bodies of authority.

Our Founders, those who ordered our arrangement of governance, built atop the works of the Enlightenment Philosophers, and each was made capable by Time itself of collectively thrusting into action both the sovereignty of the individual (John Locke, 1632-1704) and the separation of powers within government (Baron de Montesquieu, 1689-1716). We need to know this because if We are ignorant of from where We have come, then We shall know not where We are headed.

We need to fly high these words of President Woodrow Wilson:

> *Do you never stop to reflect just what it is that America stands for? If she stands for one thing more than another, it is for the sovereignty of self-governing peoples...*[32]

In short, We will "put forth new Exertions and proportion our Efforts to the Exigency of the Times", or We shall surrender our Right to determine our path.

We, as individuals and as a people, can either with haste come to appreciate Sovereignty, and Allegiance, or We can agree to a national existence predicated upon an insidious perpetuation of overwhelmed obliviousness. The Choice, thanks to our Unalienable Right of Free Will, is ours.

Time it is for us to rightly evaluate how We think and act relative to our common goals.

IX

Liberty

Liberty, according to my Metaphysicks, is an intellectual Quality. An attribute, that belongs not to Fate nor Chance. Neither possesses it, Neither is capable of it. There is nothing moral or immoral in the Idea of it. The definition of it, is a Self Determining Power, in an intellectual Agent. It implies, Thought, and Choice, and Power. It can elect between Objects, indifferent in point of Morality; neither morally good nor morally evil.[33]

– John Adams

It is an absolute that this Nation was founded upon a philosophy declaring that We, the People, are competent to the point of acting as keepers of both ourselves and the Public Liberty. Therefore, accountability is ours alone, and if – as one – We become incapable of realizing our responsibilities, if We fail to act per our sovereignties, then no souls but our own shall We have to blame when the bulwarks used to protect our many Freedoms and Rights collapse.

If We are to know not the exactness of purpose woven within "Liberty, according to my Metaphysicks…," then just as when a monarch lets slip their crown, We ought not to be surprised to find ourselves awash in the repercussions of irresponsible unawareness. We ought not to be surprised that political instability follows and that a new form of Government awaits, that Power has shifted, that economic chaos runs wild, and that international relations break down.

Rest assured, adjudication has limits, and the day is looming in which We shall find not a court capable, only a prince or princess quite eager, to hear our case of self-depredation. Time it is for us to understand that Liberty does indeed "[imply] Thought, and Choice, and Power," so much so that plain now is the error of President Jefferson's "Life, Liberty, and the pursuit of Happiness."

We the People possess a single Unalienable Right – the Liberty of "Thought, and Choice" and the consequential "Power" that follows.

Hence, We need to comprehend that within the deliberate construct of our Nation, seeing as We are naturally no different than any others, The Unalienable Endowment of Liberty is supposed to be accompanied by quite a many privileges of the alienable sort – Freedoms and Rights that have been buttressed by even more universal truths painstakingly uncovered so as to be wisely built upon by and for the benefit of future generations. We must appreciate the difference between Unalienable and alienable because the latter are vulnerable – dependent upon our rightful application of the former.

But We need not strain to see that Freedoms and Rights, including "Life" and "the pursuit of Happiness," are the result of decisions made – the desirous expressions of a people to better cope. Time itself has exposed the fact that it is the exponential application of Free Will, the bestowed ability to think and then to choose – the inevitable product of Knowledge as it is combined with Character and Experience and Condition – that ultimately determines the extent to which any collection of individuals shall enjoy the many alienable Freedoms and Rights.

Fact is, only through the derived Power of our continuous action – the evolving manifestation of our thoughts and our choices – do We make all our Freedoms and Rights possible.

Furthermore, there exists a linear logic in this matter – reasoning whereby Allegiance becomes necessitated, wherein Duty is real, and whereof Care and Prudence are inextricably allied to the Public Liberty. No, this is not to say that the outcomes of Liberty can or ought to be the same for all – for Private Liberty would cease to exist if such were so – but that the person who looks to impose their own Free Will upon the Liberty of another outside the guidelines of Negligence and Duty is either a hypocrite or a non-believer.

It is not enough to attest to a belief in Liberty, to verbally pledge Allegiance. You are either a guardian of Free Will, or you are a supporting actor in the service of the ancient hierarchy of darkness – the reprehensible caste system of this world replete with ever-evolving serfs and a mounting count of urbanized peasants that are inextricably anchored to their fruitless labors, not to mention slaves – and We each need answer as to which side We are on.

Our day is at hand.

So, if Liberty indeed be our guide, We must affix our Political Economy to Free Will, and We the Reasonable People need to sail in nonstop Pursuit of our central endeavor – the variably defined and oh-so-elusive objective of Happiness. We must center ourselves around "Thought, and Choice, and Power". In other words, with consideration given to the proper definition of Virtue – the ability to stay close to the middle points between the two extremes of Defect and Excess – and even though satisfying it might be to think our minds original, We need to look again to Aristotle and his words some 2,100 years before our American Revolution, to Ethics:

> *Happiness, then, is something final and self-sufficient, and is the end of action.*

> *…we have practically defined happiness as a sort of good life and good action.*[34]

Assuming "a sort of good life and good action" to be both beyond the need for explanation and sufficiently capable of shedding more than enough light upon the words of Adams and Jefferson, We must turn our attention toward the phrase "the end of action". It is here where We can link President Adams's metaphysics to the explicitness in his words, "the happiness of society is the end of government...". Here is where rests the relationship between general understanding and the logic within Power, the logic of Thought and Choice. It is here where We can begin to identify the ties connecting Virtue to Happiness.

Let us continue with *Ethics*:

...it is from the same causes and by the same means that every virtue is both produced and destroyed, and similarly every art; for it is from playing the lyre that both good and bad lyre-players are produced. And the corresponding statement is true of builders and of all the rest; men will be good or bad builders as a result of building well or badly. For if this were not so, there would have been no need of a teacher, but all men would have been born good or bad at their craft. This, then, is the case with the virtues also; by doing the acts that we do in our transactions with other men we become just or unjust, and by doing the acts that we do in the presence of danger, and being habituated to feel fear or confidence, we become brave or cowardly.

The same is true of appetites and feelings of anger; some men become temperate and good-tempered, others self-indulgent and irascible, by behaving in one way or the other in the appropriate circumstances. Thus, in one word, states of character arise out of like activities.

Virtue, then, being of two kinds, intellectual and moral, intellectual virtue in the main owes both its birth and its growth to teaching (for which reason it requires experience and time), while moral virtue comes about as a result of habit... From this it is also plain that none of the moral virtues arises in us by nature; for nothing that exists by nature can form a habit contrary to its nature. For instance the stone which by nature moves downwards cannot be habituated to move upwards, not even if one tries to train it by throwing it up ten thousand times; nor can fire be habituated to move downwards, nor can anything else that by nature behaves in one way be trained to behave in another. Neither by nature, then, nor contrary to nature do the virtues arise in us; rather we are adapted by nature to receive them, and are made perfect by habit.[35]

Irrespective of any personal beliefs We may individually hold regarding the origin of Free Will and or distinctions between the brain and the soul – all are irrelevant within the strict context of this world – most of us have been shortsighted in simply equating Virtue with morality. Virtue encompasses the entire whole of categorized Thought and subsequent Choice, and lest unawareness is to be our guide, our Happiness or lack thereof is ultimately connected to our desire to distance ourselves from the many Intellectual and Moral extremes.

Virtue is choosing to act in accordance with The Middle Points of Life, where We the People are sure to find Care and Prudence close by.

We must, therefore, understand that the Intellectual side of Virtue involves our traits related to our abilities of Reason, while the Moral side of Virtue concerns the predispositions of our "habits" as they are constructed around our past choices. We must appreciate this difference, even if differentiating between that which is Intellectual and that which is Moral seems trifling. Only then will We be able to embrace Adams' "intellectual quality" of Liberty as it relates to our charge of being keepers of ourselves and the Public Liberty.

And is it not foolish to suppose either a person or a people capable of consistent advancement without Intellectual Virtue? Is it not difficult to imagine anyone steadfastly improving upon their station without Reason?

Truth is – Reason, i.e., Intellectual Virtue, individually and collectively alike, is the best method to rightly address the flaws within our "state of character", and if the Power of Liberty is to be sustained it shall be done so by elevating our "intellectual and moral" Virtues.

As to the "final and self-sufficient" characteristic of Happiness, it is the fleeting nature of this "end of action" that beckons us now and again to slow down and contemplate the bigger picture of our lives – to reassess the structures of our System as well as our place therein. If We are uninterested in doing so, if We insist upon continuing to disregard the Power of reasoned Thought and Choice – if We fail to maintain the vital links between Liberty and Virtue and Happiness – then "stupid" is how We will be remembered for having chosen to hope for a Government up to the task of withstanding the tests of Time.

This day, our charge is evident and uncomplicated. We need to shepherd a proper Renaissance of Liberty. We need to usher in an awakening of "Thought, and Choice, and Power" for all to witness. Unfortunately, if We, the Reasonable People, are not up to this task, we must prepare ourselves to watch our System transform into something that We wish not to see. The Choice is ours.

Exactly what shall We do with our Liberty from this day forward?

X

Guiding Principles

Americanism means the virtues of courage, honor, justice, truth, sincerity, and hardihood – the virtues that made America. The things that will destroy America are prosperity-at-any-price, peace-at-any-price, safety-first instead of duty-first, the love of soft living and the get-rich-quick theory of life.[36]

– Theodore Roosevelt

We the People have developed a very bad case of bad habits, and no one should be taken aback by our being broached within a sea of confusion – inundated with the self-damnings of doubt and disdain and disgust while awaiting the next wave of tumult – even giving credence to money-grubbing charlatans in a desperate attempt to plug the gaping hole left by leadership's void. Therefore, with a righteous appreciation of Liberty and its indivisible bond to Happiness, with tip-of-the-hat acknowledgments to Care and Prudence along with requisite salutes to Duty, and now aware of the inseparable bindings of Virtue and Allegiance, let us not misjudge the obligations of our calling.

Agreed, one would be right to ask if We are up to such a noble venture. It does seem like We may no longer be capable of recognizing our depreciation of the things We ought to value. We, the People, do appear content playing a part in a quickening moment. Still, while there can be little doubt that We have for too long prized "the things that will destroy America", and while We have failed to demand very much from our collected Captain, it is hard to imagine We do not possess a lingering ability to alter our direction.

Suppose for a moment that We can agree with the idea that We have only ourselves to hold to account for what We ought to value and what We ought not to value. And suppose that a supermajority of us, let's say 65%, are willing to embrace the rationality of the Reasonable Person as a duty-bound advocate for "the common good of the society". If We are eager to do so, then We surely still possess the wherewithal needed to train our exertions and to harness the consequential Power of "the virtues that made America".

Then again, if We are uninterested in agreeing as to our obligations, if We are unable to identify the fibers of our decisions as each is naturally interlaced through the threads of our existence, odds are that our day has passed.

We must, together, choose to act in the name of Duty – to strive to improve ourselves and our Republic by prizing "the virtues of courage, honor, justice, truth, sincerity, and hardihood."

Likewise, in this age of instant information wherein so easy it is to lose oneself amid an unending onslaught of influences, We can rest assured that the classical wisdom of Aristotle will be instrumental in our quest to leave our troubled waters behind. Aye, best suited We will be to succeed if We constantly remind ourselves that (a) "Virtue, then, is a state of character concerned with choice, lying in a mean" and (b) "Virtue must have the quality of aiming at the intermediate".

Our "state of character" may this day be lacking, but it is only ourselves that can keep us from changing course and flying from our mastheads these words of President Adams:

Public Virtue cannot exist in a Nation without private, and public Virtue is the only Foundation of Republics.[37]

Truth is – The extremes have never offered any solace of long last. If We continue to shrink from Virtue – Private and or Public – if We insist upon valuing "the love of soft living and the get-rich-quick theory of life" while discounting the many high-caliber qualities allied to hard work, if We continue to allow our modest desire to merely have "the chance to work hard at work worth doing" to be permanently pirated by those hungry for

Power and or the Monied Interests, if We choose to scuttle our American Dream, then our System will not withstand the unforgiving tides of Time. This is what should haunt all of us.

Therein lies the fear and insecurity cast upon our lives and the storm clouds awaiting our generations to follow – the reality that a dream lost is too often a dream gone forever. We all have good reason to wonder if our moment is fading.

Having therefore arrived at this place, the intersection of Private Virtue and Public Virtue, We are confronted by our supreme dilemma – our everlasting requirement to resolve the disparities sure to exist between our individual thoughts and shared choices. Let us not be so intolerant that We fail to comprehend the wisdom within these words dated 1792, sent by President Washington to Alexander Hamilton:

> *Differences in political opinions are as unavoidable as, to a certain point, they may perhaps be necessary; but it is to be regretted, exceedingly, that subjects cannot be discussed with temper on the one hand, or decisions submitted to without having the motives which led to them, improperly implicated on the other: and this regret borders on chagrin when we find that Men of abilities – zealous patriots – having the same general objects in view, and the same upright intentions to prosecute them, will not*

exercise more charity in deciding on the opinions,
& actions of one another.[38]

As has always been the case and shall always be so long as our System is afloat, We must meld our many differences. We the People have to bring together distinctions in rural and urban ways of thinking, divergent beliefs of faith and religion and moral convictions, both general and decided disagreements regarding the scope of government, conflicting visions of our proverbial place in this world, as well as other things past and present. These are the genuine differences that must be resolved within the construct of our Government if it is to function as designed.

And besides being related to Washington's "chagrin", these are the same difficulties that tore Adams and Jefferson apart. Much is there for us to learn from the conjoined experiences and wise words of our 2nd and 3rd Presidents.

Smart We would be to ensure that our classrooms provide each student with a sound appreciation of the relationship between John Adams and Thomas Jefferson – for their bond is our bond – marked in Time by an immediate closeness borne of revolution that somehow managed to be fractured by a buildup of bitterly entwined opposition over the course of our first presidential administrations. And We should also know that their friendship was rekindled later in their lives – mutual appreciation must have been unavoidable – and that "Thomas Jefferson still survives" is rumored to have been Adams' final dying words when, in fact, Jefferson had died a few hours earlier.

Perfectly, John Adams and Thomas Jefferson passed on July 4, 1826, the 50th anniversary of our Declaration of Independence.

Fact is, the relationship between our 2nd and 3rd Presidents is arguably the best representation of the definitive dilemma within our political experiment – the act of Reconciliation – and We are altogether ignorant if We fail to value it as such. The indispensable bond between Adams and Jefferson – their status among our Founding Fathers undisputed – epitomizes the difficulty of holding together the unavoidable diversity of thoughts and choices within any Democracy.

We, the People, must understand that reconciled compromise – what Adams and Jefferson could not accomplish once governing became their reality – is what allows our Political Economy to perpetually navigate both calm and stormy seas alike. This is quite simple, seeing as We are of many and our Captain not singular, and too that Time these days moves unforgivably fast.

Reconciliation is the only deck upon which our intended structure of Government can effectively function, and an efficient structure of Economy confidently plan.

We must here be clear. It is the utmost Duty of the entrusted to reconcile what ought to be considered our coveted differences – to lead as close as is possible to the aggregated center, within the accepted margins of Liberty and Justice. We cannot afford to be pulled in one direction or another by forces existing outside of Virtue's grasp.

If those We entrust are incapable of reconciling our differences – either because of narrow convictions, selfish concerns, or other more nefarious reasons – then they have failed in their responsibilities as our Captain, and We of the crew have failed as democratic voters.

It is our Duty to avoid the troubles that plagued Adams and Jefferson, to look beyond our differences, and to diligently strengthen our commonalities, for even with their stubborn differences they would have agreed with the following declaration put forth by the man elected to the presidency almost an entire century after Jefferson's contentious victory over Adams, President McKinley:

Our differences are policies; our agreements, principles.[39]

This is paramount. Our Nation's purpose is to first convert the Liberty of many into governing principles and then to convert these principles into workable policies. If We cannot understand this, we are doomed to an undesirable destiny.

Moreover, We as one must be able to look back and understand that the partisan tension among our Founders was such that Jefferson himself was compelled to use the occasion of his inauguration to deliver these timeless words concerning the principles that unite us:

About to enter, fellow citizens, on the exercise of duties which comprehend every thing dear and valuable to you, it is proper you should understand what I deem the essential principles of our government, and consequently those which ought to shape its administration. I will compress them within the narrowest compass they will bear, stating the general principle, but not all its limitations. – Equal and exact justice to all men, of whatever state or persuasion, religious or political: – peace, commerce, and honest friendship with all nations, entangling alliances with none: – the support of the state governments in all their rights, as the most competent administrations for our domestic concerns, and the surest bulwarks against anti-republican tendencies: – the preservation of the General government in its whole constitutional vigor, as the sheet anchor of our peace at home, and safety abroad: a jealous care of the right of election by the people, a mild and safe corrective of abuses which are lopped by the sword of revolution where peaceable remedies are unprovided: – absolute acquiescence in the decisions of the majority, the vital principle of republics, from which is no appeal but to force, the vital principle and immediate parent of the despotism: – a well disciplined militia, our best reliance in peace, and for the first moments of war, till regulars may relieve them: – the supremacy of the civil over the military authority: – economy in the public expence, that labor may be lightly burthened: – the honest payment of our debts and sacred preservation of the public faith: – encouragement of agriculture, and of commerce as its handmaid: – the diffusion of information, and arraignment of all abuses at the bar of the public reason: – freedom of religion; freedom of the press; and freedom of person, under the protection of the Habeas Corpus: – and trial by juries impartially selected. These principles form the bright constellation, which has gone before us and guided our steps through an age of revolution and reformation. The wisdom of our sages, and blood of our heroes have been devoted to their attainment: – they should be the creed of our political faith; the text of civic instruction, the touchstone by which to try the services of those we trust; and should we wander from them in moments of error or of alarm, let us hasten to retrace our steps, and to regain the road which alone leads to peace, liberty and safety.[40]

Seeing as it has been far too easy for our Captain to "wander" – to lose sight of our navigational beacons – We the People mustn't be confused about Jefferson's principles. We have absolutely no choice but to acknowledge these principles – those that "form [our] bright constellation" – as being of Virtue and representing a guiding commonality within the framework of our Constitution. We must agree that Jefferson was right to say that his principles "should be the creed of our political faith," since these are the actual standards that bind us together as a Nation.

In a word, the history that We the Reasonable People will write in the coming days is sure to reflect what we have learned from "the wisdom of our sages, and blood of our heroes", not the least of which are the principles that "guided our steps through an age of revolution and reformation." Our ability to successfully attack our exigencies will undoubtedly be linked to our acknowledgment of the cyclical natures of Virtue and Vice, the paths of which determine our principles and in turn our policies and, ultimately, our habits – the harbingers of Thought and Choice.

XI

Virtuous Cycles of Endeavor

Dependence begets subservience and venality, suffocates the germ of virtue, and prepares fit tools for the designs of ambition.[41]

– Thomas Jefferson

It should be evident to each of us that our troubles extend far beyond any cursory view. We should be able to acknowledge that our problems have been compounding in Time, ever since the destination We desire was first explored, long before our Nation came into being. Our troubles are of humanity's eternal current of necessitated choices that seems to flow ever-faster – the regenerated details related to how We can best attain Happiness and Safety, the two overarching issues confronted by our Founders in their quest "to form a more perfect union."

We should by now appreciate the Preamble to our Constitution:

We the People of the United States, in Order to form a more perfect Union, establish Justice, insure domestic Tranquility, provide for the common defence, promote the general Welfare, and secure the Blessings of Liberty to ourselves and our Posterity, do ordain and establish this Constitution for the United States of America.[42]

"Blessings of Liberty" and "do ordain and establish" are heady phrases. Hence, if We of this developed day do indeed value Justice – if We understand Negligence and Duty, and if We are essentially of the same mind regarding our Guiding Principles and the more significant lessons of Time passed – then We ought by now be able to acknowledge the errors of our ways, and then tack in the direction of our proper goals.

We should be willing to ensure that our contemporary Captain is committed to strengthening our foundations and converting our principles into workable policies. We should be prepared to demand virtuous decisions from those We entrust.

Can We not appreciate the lack of room for disagreement within the Accords of Virtue – the inevitable actions borne of rightful principles and just policies – the habits inherent to sustained progress? Are We incapable of discussing how We might assemble Virtuous Cycles of Endeavor?

As Aristotle would agree, the reinforced qualities of good decisions, private and in terms of public policy alike, are of Virtue, just as Virtue is both predisposed to exceptional habits and persuaded by effectual intellect. The same can be said of the inverse. There is a persistent undercurrent of relative Dysfunction that is sure to negatively influence the outcomes borne of Vice, bad habits, and scarcity of mind.

There is a cyclical bond between our habits and Virtue and Vice – the virtuous and the vicious – and if We cannot ensure that our Political Economy promotes Virtue, then our troubles, as chosen, are just beginning.

Accordingly, We need to be wise enough to place Moral Virtue and Intellectual Virtue prominently among our primary instruments of bearing. We must remember that the choices confronting us today were, in their essence, first contemplated by many a philosopher and leader of yesteryear. We need to recognize that amongst the timeless contributions of Aristotle are included the titles *Metaphysics* and *Politics* – the former We can only imagine beckoned President Adams' definition of Liberty, while *Politics* concerns the greater community and is in large part applicable to our debates today. But let us not yet depart from our oft-cited *Nichomachean Ethics*, since the following is essential to our understanding:

Again, of all the things that come to us by nature we first acquire the potentiality and later exhibit the activity (this is plain in the case of the senses; for it was not by often seeing or often hearing that we got these senses, but on the contrary we had them before we used them, and did not come to have them by using them); but the virtues we get by first exercising them, as also happens in the case of the arts as well. For the things we have to learn before we can do them, we learn by doing them, e.g. men become builders by building and lyre players by playing the lyre; so too we become just by doing just acts, temperate by doing temperate acts, brave by doing brave acts.

This is confirmed by what happens in states; for legislators make the citizens good by forming habits in them, and this is the wish of every legislator, and those who do not effect it miss their mark, and it is in this that a good constitution differs from a bad one.[43]

Assuming then that We have some degree of appreciation for Virtue and that our Nation is one of laws, as is purported, it should be easy for us to see the relevance of "legislators make the citizens good by forming habits in them" as well as the truth within "it is in this that a good constitution differs from a bad one." Remember, the aims of our Constitution are Happiness and Safety, and our way to Happiness, as was charted by our

Founders, is to remain forever committed to a national life of Legislative Virtue.

In other words, if We possess a righteous appreciation for Liberty and Care and Prudence, along with Allegiance to our cause, then We should be able to recognize the basis of that at which We aim, and We should always be prepared to demand that the entrusted lead thusly. We should always be ready to pressure those We entrust into carrying out their Duty.

Irrespective of the rising difficulties of command within our ideal of society – free as it is and wherein there exists a natural dispute between Private Liberty and Public Liberty, wherein Reconciliation is a tall order – We should by now be able to correct our course. We should be willing to ensure that our collected Captain keeps our armada on a path of effectual moderation.

Therefore, if We are to refocus ourselves, We need first turn toward Private Liberty before directing our attention upon a proper assemblage of Public Liberty, and We need to do so from the perspective of our Captain.

We need to ask ourselves: What, within the realm of our Political Economy, is our most important personal habit of good Character that those We entrust should attempt to influence positively?

The answer is simple, as it lies within what We expect of our System: "the chance to work hard at work worth doing." The entrusted need to begin thinking and choosing consistent with what has been and forever should be good. Our Captain must embrace the essence of our humble dream and affirm via legislation the truth that is "far and away the best prize that life offers."

Time it is for us to respectfully add to the "bright constellation" of our Guiding Principles these words of President James Garfield:

> *If the power to do hard work is not Talent, it is the best possible substitute for it.*[44]

If the entrusted are worth their salt – if they really do want our efforts to be contributory and our engines to constantly churn – then it should be an effortless task for them to go about codifying the importance of our "power to do hard work".

To be sure, there are those amongst us longing to diminish the notion that working hard is a precondition on the pathway to Independence, but there are not many willing to openly stand in opposition to a doctrine holding that "dependence begets subservience and venality, suffocates the germ of virtue".

This is relatively straightforward. If for no other reason than We are all bodies in motion and the gravitational pull of the vicious is difficult to overcome, our hardworking efforts must always be aligned to a reasonably modest standard of living relative to the norm of our society. Just look about – the intergenerational influences of bad habits are all too natural, entropy is all too real, and Ignorance is not our friend.

Lest We wish to invite the conditions that history knows to threaten our System, specifically the many societal ills stemming from high levels of economic in-equality, We must make sure that our labors are forever worthwhile.

We must pressure the entrusted into exerting some authentic leadership – leadership consistent with "the virtues we get by first exercising them" – for there is no other reasonable option but to gather the political will required to guarantee an honorable appreciation of "work worth doing." We must make sure that the entrusted embrace this unsophisticated good sense of President Lincoln:

Every man is proud of what he does well; and no man is proud of what he does not do well. With the former, his heart is in his work; and he will do twice as much of it with less fatigue. The latter performs a little imperfectly, looks at it in disgust, turns from it, and imagines himself exceedingly tired. The little he has done, comes to nothing, for want of finishing.[45]

While it should go without saying that not all activities can be of the same value, and there need always be realistic expectations regarding the outcomes of what one can do well, it should be abundantly clear that doing something well within the construct of an admirable society is of Virtue and that doing something well should serve as a launching point for some measure of Opportunity.

Likewise, as every respectable Captain knows, even when the difficulties of good stewardship become complicated by a crowded intersection of individual autonomy and managerial control, having each of the crew in a position where as many as possible are doing something well is the most fundamental of tools utilized by effective leadership.

Those We entrust should by now know that our being good at something within the just boundaries of our competitive society is the natural place upon which our Free Will most often thrives. Nevertheless, so our words are not misunderstood, our thoughts not misconstrued, and so that We may turn our attention toward the horizon, let us be clear…

We deem the intentional devaluing of our "power to do hard work" to be a direct assault upon both the characteristics that make us individually strong and the very foundations of our Nation. This is painfully true in instances where work that should be available to us is presented to people with standards of living grossly mismatched against our own so that profits can be pursued within a scheme of investment wherein We have little to no interest, wherein the mechanical workings of our society are effectively manipulated.

No, We must not dwell upon the past, but there cannot be any confusion about our distrust of our Captain.

We have seen far too many factional leaders, pundits, and other persons pushing policies of encouragement for the monied at the expense of our ability to pursue our American Dream. Our trust has been withering for many a year, far longer for some, because of the policies

We have seen enacted that fail to measure up to our Guiding Principles.

However, there is one thing we have all come to expect...

The mainstream of the Monied Interests and their merchants seek to manipulate our System for their own gain – they do not possess a Care about our endeavors or our "general Welfare." They have been proven to be unconcerned with the "Posterity" of anyone but themselves and their lineage. It is ultimately the deal; the bigger, the better – their satisfying sale of anything inflated regardless of locale and irrespective of tangibility – that is their sole concern.

A critical mass of the monied wants to increase their cache of riches, never mind Virtue and Vice and "the Blessings of Liberty", and it is thusly no small matter that We need come to comprehend the following words of President Jefferson:

> *...the truth is that Capital may be produced by industry, and accumulated by economy; but juglers only will propose to create it by legerdemain tricks with paper.*[46]

Do the monied not seek ever fatter transactions of their magical Money Supply, and with each of their "legerdemain tricks with paper" do they not stuff their sacks with increased Power as well as our amplified hopes and other dependencies?

Time it is that We rise together and gain control of the methods by which these falsely crowned heads fuel their ways, for their blazes eventually consume themselves, leaving the People to ponder a sudden decline in the value of our assets along with significantly diminished prospects – each atop the burdens of layered debt and the guilt associated with how We could have let such a situation happen. In their pile of ashes is the growing collection of our dreams.

So, We must say to those of you having padded your pockets by making a mockery of our System – not the least of which are you Princes of Ponzi, whether illegal or not, and you hypocritical Frauds of Faction, whether elected or not – your engineered benefit is short-sighted and your legacy a disgrace. Chic as you may well suppose yourself, forever known you shall be for the paper you hoarded, the coins you plundered, and the self-serving Power you put into your pocket – you are no better than the traitors of old. Make amends for the benefit of yourself and your Nation – if you consider yourself a citizen – and understand that our patience grows short.

Far too many a year has passed since "aggregated capital" was the articulated concern of President Grover Cleveland:

The laboring classes constitute the main part of our population. They should be protected in their efforts to assert their rights when endangered by aggregated capital, and all statutes on this subject should recognize the care of the State for honest toil, and be framed with a view of improving the condition of the workingman.[47]

High Time it is for us to agree that "aggregated capital" is the principal obstacle within most Corridors of Opportunity – it is the yoke of unbridled capitalism and the primary barrier to our American Dream.

We need this day to acknowledge that the intentions of the falsely crowned heads rest outside our bounds of Care and Prudence and Duty, that their allegiance is to none but themselves, that their guiding principles are foreign to ours, and that their designs are not compatible with our need for sturdy behaviors of Virtue. Perhaps We ought to speak for a moment in their native tongue, the language of Supply and Demand…

In terms of commerce, of exchange and consumption, We own our Demand – it is of our Free Will – and this is beyond any reasonable debate so long as the construct of the discussion is our System proper, our intended Political Economy. In contrast, Supply is mainly of "aggregated capital," i.e., the means of production along with the outlets and services thereof are in no small part subject to the designs of the monied.

Thus, seeing as Supply and Demand are dependent upon one another inside the framework of capitalism, our structure of Economy is an indistinct balancing act between two countervailing bodies wherein the action of neither can be too radical lest the equilibrium of the governing Law, and our System itself, be jeopardized.

That is, our choices related to commerce are inextricably tied to the health of our Political Economy – our System is subjected to the increasing pressures of our quickened moment to the extent in which We allow "aggregated capital" to crack their whips.

On the other hand, the Law of Supply and Demand needs to be clarified in terms of our Labor. Yes, just as We possess our choices of consumption, in the end, We own our ability to work. Even the slave – if prepared to cope with the consequences – can choose not to work. And yes, We could delve into the differences between those of us operating as entrepreneurs and those of us who outright sell our Labor to Supply, but ultimately such a discourse is of little value.

Generally, and whether We are entrepreneurs or not, our compensations and the degrees to which We are removed from a controlled life are determined by our relative importance to the monied.

Alas! It should be no surprise that to the utmost degree possible the Monied Interests want to tilt the scales of Supply and Demand in their favor – they want to control both our Demand and our Labor – even if it means perverting our Political Economy. They view our respective agents of union and work as nuisances, and scant is their concern with the virtuous and the vicious or the reality that our Happiness is linked to a deft balancing of Supply and Demand.

And so it is that We can speak of a just Constitution, of Care and Prudence, and of the Accords of Virtue, but all is for naught if We fail to act upon our Duty of rightly balancing "aggregated capital" with both our Liberty of Demand and our Labor.

Truth is – Blindfolded or not – Lady Justice holds a scale consisting of Virtue's fulcrum and the two beams of our Political Economy in her outstretched grasp. More accurately, at the opposite ends of one of Justice's beams, We find our pans of political Excess and Defect, while Justice's other beam has the pans of Supply and Demand. These two beams, crisscrossed at their centers – Virtue's center – also possess the sliding counterweights of Government.

Justice is anything but singular, and our Captain has a role to play.

All our choices are connected, our economic interactions are of utmost significance, and one way or another We will come to terms with this fact. Hence, We return to our Preamble – to Tranquility and to Justice – and the tangled nature of our existence.

Time it is to realize that our Democracy is not intermittent. The decisions required of us, those related to our Government and Economy – choices that not all peoples have proven themselves capable of making – provide each of us with two distinct democratic votes. One is occasional, while the other is perpetual. We must realize that while We occasionally have the chance to cast our say regarding those who desire to represent us in Government, We possess the constant command of the cash and coin in our pockets and accounts.

Our Liberty of Demand is clout in and of itself – it is Power – as it allows us to cast ongoing votes of concern capable of pointing our armada in the economic direction of our collective choosing.

Aye, if We can strive both individually and legislatively to create Virtuous Cycles of Endeavor – economic activity wherein our Liberty of Demand is the controlling mechanism that calls forth a respectful Supply that in turn beckons our Labor that in turn increases our Demand and so on and so on and so on – then our "general Welfare" need never be subservient.

For this reason, we must focus our combined political and economic clout, the bright lights of our ability to think and choose, onto the absolute ambition of our American Dream. We must correlate our modest desire to "work hard at work worth doing" with the natural laws coalesced around that of Supply and Demand, and We must do so while ensuring that the rightful construct of our Political Economy is preserved.

Exactly what shall We do with our Liberty from this day forward?

XII

We Are The Government

– let us never forget that government is ourselves and not an alien power over us. The ultimate rulers of our democracy are not a President and Senators and Congressmen and Government officials but the voters of this country. [48]

– Franklin D. Roosevelt

Given that persistent instabilities and agitated passions are apt to coalesce and eventually render almost any elected Captain inadequate, it is understandable how days of discontent can push people to yearn for a strong leader. Even so, sooner or later, nearly all such longings run up against President Washington's words regarding "the alternate domination of one faction over another" and the consequential conditions that "gradually incline the minds of men to seek security and repose in the absolute power of an individual". This, We must never forget.

Fact is, F.D.R.'s sentiment that "the voters of this country" are "the ultimate rulers of our democracy" is not without limitation. For irrespective of any troubles, the voters of a democracy – any democracy – are in charge only to the extent that (a) they embrace the full ramifications of "[Liberty implies] Thought, and Choice, and Power", and (b) they refuse to pledge their allegiances to anyone or anything other than Liberty and Justice for All. All voters, everywhere, surrender The Unalienable Right of Thought and Choice to the extent that their allegiances are sworn to anything, or anyone, beyond the very idea of that "for which it stands".

Today, well beyond the years of Washington's Farewell Address, We should understand that our grasp upon Free Will loosens when We fail to unravel ourselves from the many deceptions and distortions calculated for the sole purpose of drawing our loyalties in the direction of one fraudulent Faction or another, God forbid some person.

We should by now know that We weaken our Government and thereby our System when We discount these words of President Adams:

> *The essence of a free government consists in an effectual control of rivalries.*[49]

Lest the allure of unconditional authority and its decided grasp is so great that We elect not to deny it – unless We are committed to seeing our political drama play itself out – We must embrace the full ramifications of "government is ourselves and not an alien power over us." In other words, We must rightly appreciate that our Power correlates to the aggregate measure of our collective desire to guarantee our individual Liberty inside our constitution of Justice.

We ought not to discount ourselves.

As a Nation – dispersed and incredibly diverse as We are – We have forged paths, willingly and unwillingly suffered, and accomplished to an extent that most people can only either dream of or remark about. We have learned lessons, fought battles, endured, bled, and attempted to correct injustices that make us a model of both good and bad to all others. While neither perfect nor even close to it – in fact, quite far from perfect and committing countless wrongs along our way – We have feared not, We have overcome challenges regardless of peril, and We have seized our days in an effort to better both our present situation and the prospects of generations to follow.

One would think that We could appreciate these words of President Garfield:

...now, more than ever before, the people are responsible for the character of their Congress. If that body be ignorant, reckless and corrupt, it is because the people tolerate ignorance,

recklessness and corruption. If it be intelligent, brave and pure, it is because the people demand those high qualities to represent them in the national legislature.[50]

Please make no mistake: When we the People refuse to acknowledge that something is amiss with our structures of Government and Economy, what follows is our fault.

It is our fault that We now further our inabilities to rise above the compounded nature of our troubles as We waste our days searching for others to blame.

It is our fault that We refuse to open our mind's eye, that We fail to see all instances in which We shrink from Duty as separate swells of distinct speed and depth – the primary determinates of the scope and threat within our next wave of tumult – the eventual combination of our seemingly singular issues so quickly fanned by winds from afar.

Indeed, it is our fault that We are numb to the fact that the struggles of humanity have come in many forms and that We are essentially ignorant of the metaphysical threats to our System.

Maybe our situation is no more complicated than these words of President Washington:

It is one of evils perhaps not the smallest, of democratical Governments that the People must feel before they will see or act[51]

Truth is – Our struggle is with the unabated nature of a meandering current that has no merciful end. Our fight is not with boogeymen or one another – it is with a devilish desire for us to be compliantly adrift so that pressure and need may be forever borne again, so that Dysfunction and crisis can be eternally nurtured in order to undermine betterment's cue of righteous effort. Our fight is with the Status Quo and its need to leave us languishing while our next wave of tumult builds in plain sight – well within the view of those starved for Power.

But try as does a defiant Status Quo to blur our vision, We do yet possess a good view of our situation, and We ought to be able to recognize our penchant to pursue recycled disagreements and other endless commotions as little more than effectual resignations of our responsibilities. We should realize that our ability to negotiate "the Exigency of the Times" largely depends on our desire to rid ourselves of the various arguments of old.

Moreover, We need to recognize that the primary weapons used at the onset of nearly every struggle are those of the past struggle and that if We continue to allow the entrusted to frame our problems through the looking glass of the known – thereby limiting us to the weapons of the Status Quo – then We shall be destined to drift within the tide of the times, awaiting an eventual wave of tumult far too fast and far too powerful to rise above.

The struggle itself – "the Exigency of the Times" – drives good leaders and determined societies to attack their problems with weapons 'til then unknown and from perches 'til then unseen. Captain, you must understand this, for you have no mandate to mire us in your obsolete policies and positions. We need to progress, to move forward.

Captain, assembled and as varied as you are, you may fancy yourself extraordinary, but you have been negligent. It is obvious that you Care little for the honest work of others – you have demonstrated hardly any regard for the sweeping propositions of our Union. We see your use of crisis and fear – your desire to divide us. We know your tomorrow is not ours, and as you count yours, We grow tired of hoping. Our reality has become very clear, and you need to know that the vast majority of us are neither willing to stand still per the decisions of poor leadership nor regretfully rest within the false refuge of absolute authority. We are as varied as you, actually far more so, and We are no longer interested in playing the role of your muted fool. The plank is at the ready. Woefully, many of us worry about those uninterested in allegory.

Those of you We have entrusted need to internalize these words of a young Abraham Lincoln, spoken as to the dangers arising in his day:

At what point then is the approach of danger to be expected? I answer, if it ever reach us, it must spring up amongst us. It cannot come from abroad. If destruction be our lot, we must ourselves be its author and finisher. As a nation of freemen, we must live through all time, or die by suicide.[52]

The moment has come for us, with a united voice, to acknowledge that while those with an ability to inflict devastating harm upon our society shall think thrice owing to the assurance of their own obliteration, and while the Monied Interests have not a desire to destroy us – their want is to mischievously milk us – each possesses a unique ability to contribute to our System's undoing simply by nurturing the Status Quo. In effect, both push us to undo ourselves.

This is not to say that We are in danger of tomorrow being awash in want and stripped of our Freedoms, but that Hope and delay are little more than resignations of responsibility and dangerous precursors to ruin.

Time it is to ready ourselves with the courage and absolute good judgment within these words of President Lincoln:

The dogmas of the quiet past, are inadequate to the stormy present. The occasion is piled high with difficulty, and we must rise – with the occasion. As our case is new, so we must think anew, and act anew.[53]

Our finest Presidents knew us well – they knew that within our ranks resides the knowledge of necessity, the wisdom of commonality, the stability of truth, the embers of optimism, the aspirations of tomorrow, and an appetite for action – they knew our abilities, as they knew Choice without Thought to be unwise and Thought without Choice to be devoid of Power.

Aye, We should not be surprised that the singular most important message from our top Presidents to us, the People, is uncomplicated and consistent: "We must rise [to] the occasion", "we must only put forth new Exertions and proportion our Efforts to the Exigency of the Times."

Will The Record show that We but shrugged as our armada was jeopardized because of an argument in the Captain's tower, because of the elected's inability to reconcile our differences in an "intelligent, brave and pure" manner? Shall We but cast blame as the framework around which our Nation was constructed shows signs of serious deterioration? Are We to ignore the errors of our ways as We are inundated by a torrent intended to bog down our Liberty and keep us from successfully navigating humanity's seas of circumstance? Will you side with "ignorance, recklessness and corruption"?

To "tolerate" or to "demand" – the Choice is always stark.

In short, we must act, for this "piled high" occasion is but another challenge along our way. We cannot rest – history does not linger in support of the weary. We cannot hope – dependence awaits those who do. We cannot submit – wretched are the kept. Impose ourselves – We must. "Think anew, and act anew" – We will.

PART
THREE

POWER

While all other Sciences have advanced, that of Government is at a Stand; little better understood; little better practiced now than 3 or 4 thousand years ago.[viii]

– John Adams

---

viii "John Adams to Thomas Jefferson, 9 July 1813," *Founders Online*, National Archives, https://founders.archives.gov/documents/Jefferson/03-06-02-0230. [Original source: *The Papers of Thomas Jefferson*, Retirement Series, vol. 6, *11 March to 27 November 1813*, ed. J. Jefferson Looney. Princeton: Princeton University Press, 2009, pp. 277–280.]

XIII

Enthroned

Behind the ostensible government sits enthroned an invisible government owing no allegiance and acknowledging no responsibility to the people. To destroy this invisible government, to befoul the unholy alliance between corrupt business and corrupt politics is the first task of the statesmanship of the day.[54]

– Theodore Roosevelt

Regarding the subject of Power, We need to turn our attention toward the certainty that Time past, along with days yet to come, when viewed fully, reveals the whole of humanity's Free Will.

We must recognize that, despite those desperate to inscribe their own versions, Time alone is both the undeniable proof of what has been and the prophetic vision of what is prone to be. Ubiquitously present and pure in truth – unmoved by those bent in pursuit of their own reality – Time is the perfect incidental observer, and We need therefore acknowledge it to be the definitive testament to the exertions of our lives as well as the complete accounting of that which is good and that which is not.

Time is the immaculate Record of Choice.

In addition, being flawlessly organized into chapters of behaviors and with bookmarks of ideas inserted relative to various realizations of Power, Time is charitable and generous. Time forever encourages us to nurture our abilities of Thought and to improve upon our decisions of Choice while it incessantly orders precedent and possibility to stand at the ready in anticipation of our commands.

Time even presents us with the bigger picture – the reality that humankind is geared to exert, that our choices are actual applications of force set against countervailing Wills looking to contest our ways, and that each society's appreciation of Free Will tends to wax and wane in conjunction with the extent to which it both shields and facilitates the Liberty of its citizens.

So it is that We have little reason to be ignorant regarding our American moment – the definitive lesson concerning the calculated conditions required to create and sustain, as well as to either improve or weaken, scales of balance capable of justly moderating different measures of human force. We should by now be wise enough to treasure the connotations packed inside of our phrase Liberty and Justice for All. We ought to understand that – even though some amongst us are quick to assert that We are naturally exceptional, that We hold a special place and have a special purpose within The Record – our United States of America illustrates the possibilities of Choice rather than any guarantee of Power.

Truth is – The ideas bound to the abutted bookmarks of our founding, the years 1776 (Declaration of Independence) and 1787 (The Constitution of the United States), are those of Free Will, of Independence, and of collected individuality – of being in command of one's own life within the reliable construct of a Representative Democracy freed from external impositions. And We should be able to see that our bookmarks, embossed with the ambitiously imperfect lives of our Forefathers, represent the embodiment of an unwavering desire to advance Liberty – that our Founding Fathers engineered their grand mechanism in order to fortify the possibilities borne of our Free Will, and they did so via the creation of "a more perfect Union."

We the People should be able to appreciate that our Nation was constructed to circulate Liberty within a specific framework of Justice wherein compatible structures of Government and Economy could each rightly facilitate "Thought, and Choice, and Power" in persons and collections thereof alike.

Furthermore, it is pretty dicey for one to be misguided in terms of Liberty and Justice, for eventually

We are each apt to find it damning to have believed a simple pledge sufficient – to be of two minds. How prudent We would be to prepare one's self to come to terms with the distinct possibility that – when all is said and done – the choices borne of our own Free Will are of preeminent importance, that there may well exist a level of expectation justly correlated to the potential bound up within our abilities, and that the Power expected of one's thoughts and choices is relative to the exponential breadth of one's reach.

It is no stretch to say that We might one day come to understand that our fate, along with any moniker of exception, rests upon the degree to which We choose these days to rightly exert the Power that We individually possess in the cause of that which is naturally good – Liberty And Justice For All.

We need not any further evidence. Time has already spoken.

Liberty and Justice are indivisible, united as one, and We can be exceptional only to the extent that We equally protect and preserve each for all. There is no other conclusion to be had regarding this matter unless We are to live lives of either Ignorance or ambivalence or both, uncaring as to the purpose of our System and its juxtaposition against the determined resolve of overwhelming Power.

We are supposed to be The Shepherds of Liberty and The Caretakers of Justice.

Now, today, if a supermajority of us can agree with Adams' definition of Liberty as it is entwined with his words concerning "ease, comfort, security," We need to train our thoughts upon a proper combination of Liberty and Justice. We must find our way within these words of President Jefferson:

> *Of Liberty then I would say that, in the whole plenitude of it's extent, it is unobstructed action according to our will: but rightful liberty is unobstructed action according to our will, within the limits drawn around us by the equal rights of others. I do not add 'within the limits of the law'; because law is often but the tyrant's will, and always so when it violates the right of an individual.*[55]

Imagine, in the not-so-distant future, Time placing another bookmark in our name – one denoting how We the People rose to the occasion and corrected our course. Would We not be required first to acknowledge the depths of injurious actions lying beneath the surface of the countless things We had codified to be "within the limits of [our] law"? Can such a day ever be possible if We do not admit our errors – if We refuse first to confess?

We must recognize both the reality that the very seed of our problems can be found within our imperfect selves – far outside the domain of that which is perfectly good – and that We jeopardize our cause when We adhere ourselves to falsehoods holding up our law as judge and jury of what is good and right, for as was the case with Jefferson himself We have been too quick for too long to turn a blind eye towards the complexities of "within limits drawn around us by the equal rights of others."

Is it not fair for one to wonder if We have abandoned our bearings of good and bad and right and wrong, to worry that We, the People, are no longer interested in the critical distinctions differing both Virtue from Vice and that which is private from that which is public? Aye, our faculties have been corrupted, and We have placed ourselves in jeopardy of being deemed unworthy standard bearers of Rightful Liberty. Our Power is in decay.

Can we not understand the genuine differences in the Power springing from Vice compared to Virtue? And is there not stability within Aristotle's words concerning Moral Virtue, i.e., "Virtue, then, is a state of character concerned with choice…it is a mean between two vices, that which depends on excess and that which depends on defect…"?

Fact is, foolish is the one who fails to identify, for example, the Virtue of Courage as the mean between the Vice of Rashness ("the rash man") and the Vice of Cowardice, and Temperance as being equally flanked by Self-Indulgence and Insensibility, Liberality by Prodigality and Avarice ("meanness"), Truthfulness by Boastfulness and False Humility ("mock-modest people"), and too that Righteous Indignation is the mean between Envy and Spitefulness.[ix] Only a fool would declare the Power of a virtuous one no different than that of one clothed in the many excesses and defects of personal Character.

Should We strike Discernment from our vocabulary?

Assuming that We value both "the rights of the individual" and "the equal rights of others" – that We genuinely believe in Free Will, and Justice, for all – do We not also have to distinguish Private Liberty from Public Liberty?

After all, and in the plainest of terms, Envy, Anger, and Lust are private affairs of Thought unless a Choice is made that impacts another person – e.g., theft, assault, harassment, or some broken vow – Gluttony and Sloth are of Choice and can be private only up to the point at which the marketplace and our governing rules thereof intervene, Greed by its very definition is the unjust accumulation of resources and therefore is of a public nature, and of course Pride – slithering back and forth between public and private – always looking for an opportunity to wed itself to our other flaws of Character in order to execute any a Choice capable of placing some degenerative weight upon any good scale of balance.

---

ix   Warren, Street R. "Aristotle's Virtues and Vices." *Course Materials PSY 461*, Central Washington University, Ellensburg, WA 98926-7575, 2016, www.cwu.edu/~warren/Unit1/aristotles_virtues_and_vices.htm. [Original Source: Aristotle (1955). *The Ethics of Aristotle: The Nichomachaen Ethics.* (rev. ed.) (J. K. Thomson, trans.). New York: Viking. p. 104.]

None of this is complicated. Agreed, a mean of Character is difficult to determine, and that which separates public from private can hide within the minutiae of a lone, solitary heartbeat – but deep down, We do know the fundamentals of what is good and right, and We ought to be able to acknowledge that We degrade ourselves and our System when We pursue paths that either neglect to respect the private "rights of the individual" or steer clear of the imperfections within our own unfinished Character.

We ought to be able to agree that deeds running afoul of Rightful Liberty are both borne of bad choices and likely to feed the cancerous strains within our society. We ought to be able to comprehend that the choices We make along our way constitute the evidence of our lives, and We ought to guard against being deceived.

Know this – The debasement of Liberty and the degradation of Justice is how those opposed to our mission carry out their objectives, and unless We shall acquiesce as our Government and or our Economy are altered to the liking of those so corrupted, We must be up to the task of keeping their "unholy alliance" at bay.

Unless the idea of edicts and thrones suits us, We must forever work to strengthen our unsteady scales of balance and to neutralize the things that flank our path to good – The Excesses of Unabashed Freedoms and The Defects of Regimented Rights – Power Run Amuck.

XIV

In Good Faith

Power always sincerely, conscientiously, de tres bon Foi, believes itself Right. Power always thinks it has a great Soul, and vast Views, beyond the Comprehension of the Weak.[56]

– John Adams

We, the People, have yielded to those wanting to transform our System into the stage upon which the wedding of two of humanity's most irreverent traits is best officiated. We have obediently bowed in attentive silence as the marriage of Greed to Pride has been deemed acceptable, and We ought not to be surprised that We must now turn our attention towards "the limits of [our] law".

Truth be told, and with no thanks to the Monied Interests and their funding of our dysfunctional politics, our better senses have been rubbed so raw that We have allowed our structures of Government and Economy to be corrupted under the cover of our laws. As a people, We have become indifferent regarding those possessing both a disregard for Virtue and a fixation upon their ability to tip any a scale to their favor – the more the better, including complete control of the scale itself.

We have been allowing ourselves to be effectually shackled – powerless, as the sordid ways of toxic Vice romp about within the fertile grounds of our Political Economy. We have surrendered much of our Liberty, the Unalienable Right of Thought and Choice.

Therefore, We must sharpen our senses with an awareness of the forces working against us, and We must strengthen our positions with the gravity of our endeavors. We must resolutely object to those who adulterate our System.

We the People need to concern ourselves with the Monied Interests.

The Monied Interests, devoted as they are to that which they in their minds so richly deserve – all those possessing little respect for any balance aside from that of their ledgers – they see us as barely more than numbers to be plied per their desires, debits and credits alike.

The Monied Interests, with their many offspring in tow – all those of this world far less concerned with the things that must be good in as much as they are focused upon advancing their positions and acquiring their next measure of Power – they are why We can no longer afford to bite our tongues and pray for a better day.

Time it is for us to acknowledge that those of Greed and Pride have long concealed their disdain for many of the wise words left us by our sages, not the least of which are these of President Jefferson:

> *I hope we shall… crush in it's birth the aristocracy of our monied corporations which dare already to challenge our government to a trial of strength, and to bid defiance to the laws of their country.*[57]

So that We may harness our actions to best exert the weight of our exponential Power, Time it is for us to recognize our balancing act and then harmonize our choices as We shove aside all distractions. Aye, Time it is for us, those who believe in Liberty and Justice for All, to embrace the reality that our agent of work, our Economy, transcends our agent of union, our Government. And that by way of literal definitions, it is the productive management of our resources that prefigure our arrangement of political institutions, laws, and customs through which We bring about the necessary functions of governing.

In other words, if We want our Nation to be durable and free, then We must agree that the natural platform for our Union rests within the trading of the produce of our labors along with our selling of our own labors – our choices must reflect this reality. Economy is the beam on which We live; Government is the axiomatic equalizer. Likewise, if Free Will is to reign over our structures, then our attachments of commonality must always be intertwined with our productive endeavors and the good habits required thereof.

However, and though its foremost importance might suggest otherwise, no one should suppose that the workings of Economy can supplant either the workings of Government or alliances of Safety. Any replacement of any function of Government, or Safety, with means of Economy represents nothing less than a partial takeover of our Union.

As to harmonizing our positions along our beam, if We can agree regarding the critical nature of Economy and the utmost relevance of "work worth doing," then in general terms, We should also be able to agree as to what We ought to expect from those We entrust. Those of us valuing our Unalienable Right of Free Will, different as We are, should be able to agree regarding the need for our Captain to moderate any excessive weight applied by Greed and or Pride to our System – to be forever prepared to utilize our counterweights, i.e., the ballasts of good governance.

Fact is, our Founders did not intend our Government to be static, and We have decisions to make regarding how our Nation shall function.

The day has come for us to either wield Liberty – to preserve the belief that "the happiness of society is the end of government" – or consent to the consequences of the many pitched battles fought by those vying to satisfy their own needs for Power. We must choose if

We want our agent of union to function according to a set of tenets consistent with this timeless statement of President Theodore Roosevelt:

> *When I say I believe in a square deal I do not mean… it possible to give every man the best hand. If the cards do not come to any man, or if they do come, and he has not got the power to play them, that is his affair. All I mean is that there shall not be any crookedness in the dealing.*[58]

Are We to merely watch as our failure to ensure a "square deal" for the whole of our citizenry continues to evolve?

Are We to accept a reality wherein our attachments of commonality continue to disintegrate because We refuse to regulate "crookedness in the dealing" with "the limits of [our] law"?

Will We continue to be willfully deceived by those who, based upon their actions, loathe the intended purpose of our Government – how the People are able to create, modify, and administer a legal basis of union that is rightly built upon Justice?

Will We permit the crushing weight of overwhelming Greed and Pride to dominate our society?

Shall We concede that Choice seldom lingers?

Yes, the Monied Interests know our quaint concept of country, but at best, they have only a passing regard for the Free Will of others. The motives of the Monied Interests, along with the machinations of their minions, are tightly wound around the devilish desires of unbridled capital – they live in a world predicated upon the predisposed Prejudices of Power, and they have hardly a Care for the vast majority of humanity or the pervasiveness of want.

But let us be perfectly clear. While no one should think that the outcomes of Liberty can be even close to the same for all, as Private Liberty would cease to exist if such were so, We cannot escape the fact that chief amongst our elections in life is the Choice between being either a Shepherd of Liberty and a Caretaker of Justice or a supporting actor within a caste system replete with ever-evolving serfs and a mounting count of urbanized peasants. Our reality is inescapable – Righteous Liberty has widespread implications for all humankind, including each personal Choice within any working Economy.

Let us no longer be deceived either by the proximity of their bull to our Lady or by the distractions that come along with but a bit of coin in our pockets and a frenetic pace of life.

If We only open our eyes, We will see that our Power is diminished with each engineered cycle of boom and bust whereby the Monied Interests manage to increase their stature – like ever-growing crowned heads upon practical thrones of influence – they somehow end up even better prepared than before to lead their companions in the production of yet another round of their concoctions designed first to placate and then altogether intoxicate us, and oh how We have preferred their brew over Virtue or any other requirement of that which must be good.

We must come to understand that of the predictable: When intoxicated, taking pleasure in the temporary high of excited inhibition and the flood of monies eagerly supplied by the deal makers and the brokers and their bosses, easy it is to discount the inevitable consequences sure to follow, for such is the certainty of the cycles powered by the Monied Interests.

Hence, no excuse do We have not to understand that save for speed and strength the dangers lurking now are no different than ever before. People have always been vulnerable to those eager to sit at the feast of Amalgamated Power – a virtual smorgasbord where those with insatiable appetites attempt to satisfy their hunger by voraciously devouring all the resources that We the People of this world ignorantly heap upon their platters. They feast upon material things as they franticly collect every crumb of communication and hoard every bit of knowledge, as they stuff all the information and influence within reach of their devolved digits into sacks for safekeeping.

Admit it – We have grown so accustomed to the touch of the tentacles that We have become compliant, attentive to the needs of those intent on corrupting our System. We have unwittingly handed over our responsibilities of Government to the controlling instincts of the Monied, "de tres bon Foi" as they so certainly are. We have been fooled into believing that those of Greed and Pride have our best interests in mind, that they operate in good faith, when in fact We have surrendered our ability to create, modify, and administer our laws – Government "of the People, by the People, for the People."[x]

And so it is that We have grown tired of acquiescing, no longer willing to accept laws and policies crafted around the false promise that our livelihoods are best served when dependent upon the opulent, if not gross, comfort of the monied few. Time it is to put aside our differences and to awaken as one.

We must realize that We are powerless when divided, and We must commit ourselves to righting the unjust pressures being exerted upon our scales of balance by electing to our chairs of Government only those individuals dedicated to reconciling our differences.

We, the People, have no Choice but to embrace Virtue and all the ramifications thereof.

---

x   Lincoln, Abraham. "The Gettysburg Address, November 19, 1863" *Abraham Lincoln Online*, 2020 Abraham Lincoln Online, http://www.abrahamlincolnonline.org/lincoln/speeches/gettysburg.htm. Gettysburg, Pennsylvania [Source: Collected Works of Abraham Lincoln, edited by Roy P. Basler et al.]

XV

Bank of Knowledge

Knowledge will forever govern Ignorance: And a people who mean to be their own Governors, must arm themselves with the power which knowledge gives.[59]

– James Madison

Exactly what within "Knowledge will forever govern Ignorance" is there not for you to agree with, and is this maxim of Madison not perfectly aligned with "Liberty, according to my Metaphysicks, is an intellectual Quality. An attribute, that belongs not to Fate nor Chance"?

Moreover, can We not agree that "a people who mean to be their own Governors" should always look to "arm themselves with the power which knowledge gives"? And does it not make sense that our Knowledge – so mercurially mixed with our Character, Experience, and Condition – is a component of our Power and worthy of our utmost attention? Are the answers to these questions not undeniable?

So, having surveyed Character, and Moral Virtue – and realizing that within our formula of Choice the variables of Experience and Condition are consistent with Merriam-Webster's definitions reading (a) "the conscious events that make up an individual life" and (b) one's current "state of being" – let us identify the essential characteristics of Liberty's "intellectual quality".

We need to arm ourselves with a proper abridgment of Knowledge per Merriam-Webster:

(1) "the fact or condition of knowing something with familiarity gained through experience or association"

(2) "the fact or condition of being aware of something"

(3) "the sum of what is known: the body of truth, information, and principles acquired by humankind"

First, consider some "familiarity [We have] gained through experience or association."

Are We the People not familiar with the fact that our Power is vulnerable to the extent that our Government is susceptible to those searching for control?

Are We not familiar with the fact that We avail ourselves to the wants of the Masters of Supply when We loosen our grasp upon our Liberty of Demand?

And are We not familiar with the fact that the specialization of work, i.e., the Division of Labor, has proven to have broad implications for the whole of human life?

Assuming We can recognize the threads relating the Division of Labor and the Masters of Supply to our Government, let us now familiarize ourselves with the words below, also dated 1776 and published in *An Inquiry into the Nature and Causes of the Wealth of Nations*, the seminal work of Scottish social philosopher Adam Smith:

> *The difference of natural talents in different men, is, in reality, much less than we are aware of; and the very different genius which appears to distinguish men of different professions, when grown up to maturity, is not upon many occasions so much the cause, as the effect of the division of labour. The difference between the most dissimilar characters, between a philosopher and a common street porter, for example, seems to arise not so much from nature, as from habit, custom, and education. When they came in to the world, and for the first six or eight years of their existence, they were, perhaps, very much alike, and neither their parents nor play-fellows could perceive any remarkable difference. About*

that age, or soon after, they come to be employed in very different occupations. The difference of talents comes then to be taken notice of, and widens by degrees, till at last the vanity of the philosopher is willing to acknowledge scarce any resemblance. But without the disposition to truck, barter, and exchange, every man must have procured to himself every necessary and conveniency of life which he wanted. All must have had the same duties to perform, and the same work to do, and there could have been no such difference of employment as could alone give occasion to any great difference of talents.[60]

Now, let us also familiarize ourselves with the fact that Smith, nearly twenty years before publishing *The Wealth of Nations*, gave us his work *The Theory of Moral Sentiments* and these following words therein:

The perfection of [policy], the extension of trade and manufactures, are noble and magnificent objects. The contemplation of them pleases us, and we are interested in whatever can tend to advance them. They make part of the great system of government, and the wheels of the political machine seem to move with more harmony and ease by means of them. We take pleasure in beholding the perfection of so beautiful and grand a system, and we are uneasy till we remove any obstruction that can in the least disturb or encumber the regularity of its motions. All constitutions of government, however, are valued only in proportion as they tend to promote the happiness of those who live under them. This is their sole use and end.[61]

What a notion! Why does it seem like We have yet to become familiar with these ideas and their relationship to our reality? Again, let us say, "All constitutions of government, however, are valued only in proportion as they tend to promote the happiness of those who live under them." Have We lost sight of who and what We are supposed to be? Do We the People no longer believe? Have We succumbed to the cynicisms birthed by Hypocrisy?

Are We of this day even capable of pursuing "the perfection of policy" as it relates to our Division of Labor and the Masters of Supply?

Alas, we have entrusted too many determined to satisfy their own wants – those looking to hide their lineages and veil their intentions amidst our alienable banners of Freedoms and Rights. We have become ambivalent regarding those with a need for control and their use of our Government as the means through which they can legally impose their Free Will upon the rest of us.

Are We not yet familiar with how those starved for Power carry out their business?

Time it is for us to acknowledge how the various Creatures of Control use disputes to turn our attention away from their actual plans because they have proven themselves eager to divide us into more manageable groups far less likely to be concerned with any idea involving "the perfection of policy". In other words, We need open our eyes to the fact that the Creatures of Control understand humanity's intrinsic desire to organize around shared interests, habits, and lifestyles – they realize We are instinctively tribal, and they always stand ready to push the buttons, flip the switches, and turn the knobs of fear and distrust.

Lest We are to deem Experience worthless, We need to admit that our Knowledge must include two critical realities: (a) We are a complicated tribe intended to be bound by a shared interest in Free Will, and (b) We are at our absolute best when vital habits of good Character propel us.

We must acknowledge the threads of our historical gyrations, and We ought not be surprised that there are those amongst us more than happy to coddle our differences, highlight all conceivable markings of clan, and capitalize on the disparities within our collective Condition. Aye, our Experience should allow us to recognize now that our troubles have much if not everything to do with our lack of desire to define and to defend our brand of tribalism, for – as we've seen – our bindings are not physical, and our exigencies are easily exacerbated by the false flags of lifestyle, clan, and Condition.

We should be able to realize that We are once again vulnerable owing to our unwillingness to recognize a simple fact: If our individual choices are our final measure, then our attachments of commonality are un-doubtedly metaphysical. We should by now be familiar with this characteristic of Liberty's "intellectual qual-ity" – our principal means of cohesion and adhesion.

As to "the fact or condition of being aware of something," can all of us not agree that Awareness – as opposed to Ignorance – is an invaluable asset requiring some degree of continuous cultivation?

Can We not acknowledge the perils dwelling within any Choice constructed atop Ignorance?

Can We not see that probability accompanies Choice and that it makes sense to favor those possibili-ties consistent with the definitions of Likely, Reliable, and Credible? Can We not see the threads connecting Awareness to the Virtue of Prudence?

How very wise We would be to heed these words of President Jefferson:

if a nation expects to be ignorant & free, in a state of civilisation, it expects what never was & never will be.[62]

Truth is – If our sages could speak with us today, they would tell us to dive deep and to garner an ap-preciation of the classical differentiation between the Moral and the Intellectual. Our sages would implore us to be aware of the inherent fragility of Awareness, and they would plead with us to acknowledge that our natural endowment of Liberty demands that We, the People, strive for outcomes predicated upon Justice.

They would tell us to cherish our ability to pursue both "the perfection of policy" and an understanding of our processes, as each is undeniably woven within our System and our Happiness.

If our sages could speak with us today, they would advise us that Freedoms and Rights are not guaranteed, and expectations otherwise have proven to be the folly of many a fool.

So it is that We return to leadership and a question for ourselves: If We as a Nation are to prize "perfection," then shouldn't We entrust only those with a sincere desire to better our Political Economy and to identify fact as fact and truth as truth? A young Lincoln framed this matter well with these words:

> *Reason, cold, calculating, unimpassioned reason, must furnish all the materials for our future support and defence.*[63]

"Reason, cold, calculating, unimpassioned reason," are these words not sufficiently clear, concise, and contrary to Ignorance?

Indeed, if our sages could speak with us today, they would implore us to embrace the deliberate details of our processes, and they would want to know why We seem so opposed to dedicating ourselves to our improvement. They would surely want to know why We have effectually accepted Ignorance. If our sages could speak with us today, they would tell us that the turbulences of life would begin to dissipate – our Power would strengthen – if We, individually and collectively alike, would dedicate ourselves to improving our Knowledge, our Character, our Experience, and our Condition.

Fortunately, We need not look back far to find reasoned process rightly related to "the perfection of policy". President Garfield, though in office for only six brief months in 1881, touched upon the nature of these waters when he said:

> *The problems to be solved in the study of human life and character are, therefore, these: Given the character of a man, and the conditions of life around him, what will be his career? Or, given his career and surroundings, what was his character? Or, given his character and career of what kind were his surroundings? The relation of these three factors to each other is severely logical. From them is deduced all genuine History. Character is the chief element, for it is both a result and a cause – a result of influences and a cause of results.*[64]

Shouldn't We by now be aware of the importance of Character and Career, and the fact that the sentiments of President Garfield regarding this matter were cursory and far from complete?

Shouldn't We know that our reservoirs of Character are filled with the accumulation of our prior "thoughts and choices" and that one's Labor (Career as labeled by

Garfield) is both a requirement and a product within our Political Economy?

Shouldn't We by now know that the opposing forces of others are constantly being applied against each of us, and that the Power of our Labor can only be fully realized when the totality of our System is sound – when our Nation is efficient – when entropy is minimized and when We have wide Corridors of Opportunity in place?

After all, seeing as most of us have some opinion about the general disagreement and the historical turmoil between Adam Smith and Karl Marx, shouldn't We have progressed beyond their chapters, along with those of Lincoln and Garfield?

Shouldn't We have already resolved many of the difficulties associated with the science of Ease and Comfort and Security?

Shouldn't our Awareness, by now, include the certainty that We cannot expect Liberty and Justice to prevail if We leave the resolves of Government and Economy to a few – if We allow Opportunity to be a traded commodity, Dysfunction an accepted afterthought – if Negligence, Care, and Prudence are to be irreverently brushed aside while Ignorance is willfully accepted – if Duty shall be jeered and Virtue found worthless – if Allegiance is to be defined by the monied and if Ponzi is to go unnoticed – if Faction is to be valued above all, Sovereignty a subordinate consideration – if We wish to discount the relationship between Knowledge and Character and Experience and Condition – if We are incapable of differentiating between that which is

Private and that which is Public – if distinguishing the Intellectual from the Moral is just too much – if Reconciliation is a hassle and Guiding Principles quaint – if Supply and Demand is over our heads – if Vice is no big deal – if the Status Quo shall rule – if We are to acquiesce to Greed and Pride as our scabs are scraped off our imperfections?

To be sure, no soul should expect Liberty and Justice to prevail if Ignorance is allowed to rule. We should be aware of this characteristic of Liberty's "intellectual quality".

Lastly, let us turn toward "the sum of what is known: the body of truth, information, and principles acquired by humankind".

Let us agree that if our subject is our Union, i.e., the embodiment of our combined strengths, weaknesses, fears, desires, beliefs, experiences, and expectations, then We must chart our national course relative to our ultimate objective of individual Happiness. But considering our size and diversity, this is quite difficult. And if We fail to place a proper valuation upon humanity's Bank of Knowledge – if Knowledge is not sufficiently dispersed – We will undoubtedly find our attachments compromised.

Let us agree that unless We are comfortable with our Armada of Liberty always struggling in unrelenting and ever more unmanageable seas, We must possess a readiness to employ the wisdom within "the sum of what is known".

For example, "the body of truth, information, and principles" We use in plotting our course should always include this 2,350-year-old tenet of Aristotle:

> *…whether happiness is to be acquired by learning or by habituation or some other sort of training, or comes in virtue of some divine providence or again by chance. Now if there is any gift of the gods to men, it is reasonable that happiness should be god-given, and most surely god-given of all human things inasmuch as it is the best. But this question would perhaps be more appropriate to another inquiry; happiness seems, however, even if it is not god-sent but comes as a result of virtue and some process of learning or training, to be among the most godlike things; for that which is the prize and end of virtue seems to be the best thing in the world, and something godlike and blessed.*[65]

Let us agree that our Pursuit of Happiness need not be overly complicated. Which is to say, if We the People would collectively strive to translate "the sum of what is known" into well-formulated policies and procedures – if We would agree to protect and to pursue the application of facts and truths and Virtue – then We would begin to instinctively invest in our Character, our Condition, and our Knowledge, in addition to our Safety, and We would thusly find our Experience to be that of progressing towards our objective.

If, as a people, We would commit to employing "the body of truth, information, and principles [thus far] acquired by humankind", then We would surely come to revere Justice for All, We would understand the many misnomers within Freedoms and Rights, We would know the simple meanings of Ease and Comfort and Security, and We would come to appreciate the unchanging nature of humankind as well as the present applicability of answers revealed long ago.

If We would focus our Pursuit of Happiness upon our Knowledge and our Experience and our Character and our Condition, then We would surely benefit from the Power borne of Rightful Liberty, and We would value these words found in Aristotle's *Politics*:

> *...Some think that a very moderate amount of virtue is enough, but set no limit to their desires of wealth, property, power, reputation, and the like. To whom we reply by an appeal to facts, which easily prove that mankind do not acquire or preserve virtue by the help of external goods, but external goods by the help of virtue, and that happiness, whether consisting in pleasure or virtue, or both, is more often found with those who are most highly cultivated in their mind and in their character, and have only a moderate share of external goods, than among those who possess external goods to a useless extent but are deficient in higher qualities; and this is not only*

matter of experience, but, if reflected upon, will easily appear to be in accordance with reason.[66]

Shouldn't We now know the importance of Character and the vast implications regarding any lack thereof? Shouldn't We understand that Choice is the undeniable charge of the ever-present and that it is our responsibility to choose if We will value the "higher qualities" of Virtue over the ways of Vice?

Let us view this issue through a more current lens. Let us pull the thread connecting Aristotle to our collective neglect vis-à-vis the following words of President Theodore Roosevelt, the latter as well acquainted as any with leadership and the manners and modes of Greed and Pride:

> *If we lose [our energetic and vigorous] qualities, and sink into a nation of mere hucksters, putting gain over national honor, and subordinating everything to mere ease of life, then we shall indeed reach a condition worse than that of the ancient civilizations in the years of their decay.*[67]

As our subject is our Union, our Bank of Knowledge must include the principle that virtuous ways are integral to sustained progress, and those We entrust must be committed to championing Virtue and the good choices thereof. We must acknowledge that only fools salute as waves of Greed and Pride build in plain sight.

Seeing as We are a complicated tribe on a quest to further humankind's ability to expand "happiness to the greatest number of persons, and in the greatest degree", our Bank of Knowledge must include a thoughtful appreciation for the complexities inherent with our structure of Government, and We must acknowledge that Private concerns can never be allowed to either constitute or control the fulcrum of our societal scales.

Seeing as We must chart a collective course founded upon our individual selves, our Bank of Knowledge must include the understanding that We cannot allow our shared interest in Rightful Liberty to be overshadowed by disagreements concerning personal habits and lifestyles. We can ill afford to have our mission sidetracked by arguments concerning what is Private and what is Public.

Fact is, irrespective of our need to always debate the precise construction of the ties that bind us, We must appreciate the reality that our attachments were formulated via our shared interest in Free Will of Thought and Choice, and then forged with the ways of Virtue as necessitated by our quest.

We must understand the metaphysics of how We are both drawn and held together – along with the reasons behind our now frayed shared interests – and We ought to be thankful for our charge as Shepherds of Liberty and Caretakers of Justice. We should by now know this characteristic of Liberty's "intellectual quality" – "[our] body of truth, information, and principles".

Be honest with yourself: What within "Knowledge will forever govern Ignorance" can you not agree with, and is this maxim of Madison not perfectly aligned with "Liberty, according to my Metaphysicks, is an intellectual Quality. An attribute, that belongs not to Fate nor Chance"?

Should not you, one of the People, "arm [yourself] with the power which knowledge gives"?

Let us close this chapter with the entire paragraph of Lincoln's "cold, calculating, unimpassioned reason":

> *They [the generation of the revolution] were the pillars of the temple of liberty; and now, that they have crumbled away, that temple must fall, unless we, their descendants, supply their places with other pillars, hewn from the solid quarry of sober reason. Passion has helped us; but can do so no more. It will in future be our enemy. Reason, cold, calculating, unimpassioned reason, must furnish all the materials for our future support and defence.; Let those materials be moulded into general intelligence, sound morality, and in particular, a reverence for the constitution and laws: and, that we improved to the last; that we remained free to the last; that we revered his name to the last; that, during his long sleep, we permitted no hostile foot to pass over or desecrate his resting place; shall be that which to learn the last trump shall awaken our WASHINGTON.*[68]

XVI

Education

Upon the subject of education, not presuming to dictate any plan or system respecting it, I can only say that I view it as the most important subject which we as a people can be engaged in. That every man may receive at least, a moderate education, and thereby be enabled to read the histories of his own and other countries, by which he may duly appreciate the value of our free institutions, appears to be an object of vital importance, even on this account alone, to say nothing of the advantages and satisfaction to be derived from all being able to read the scriptures and other works, both of a religious and moral nature, for themselves. For my part, I desire to see the time when education, and by its means, morality, sobriety, enterprise and industry, shall become much more general than at present, and should be gratified to have it in my power to contribute something to the advancement of any measure which might have a tendency to accelerate the happy period.[69]

–Abraham Lincoln

Much to the chagrin of those with little need for Nation – those who are determined to find goodness in Greed, those who believe a corporation is a human being, and all those in search of control – We do still appreciate our ability to think and choose wisely. Most of us recognize our need for Reason. We understand why our sages felt compelled to leave us with abundant wisdom concerning how societies cultivate Knowledge.

Therefore, if We are to launch our new exertions, We must explore our topic. We must affirm Merriam-Webster's definition of our subject, Education:

(1) (a) "the action or process of educating or of being educated
also: a stage of such a process"

(b) "the knowledge and development resulting from the process of being educated"

(2) "the field of study that deals mainly with methods of teaching and learning in schools"

First, We must illuminate the role Education plays within Liberty's formula. That is, assuming We can agree that our development of Knowledge is our "process of being educated" – à la Aristotle's "intellectual virtue in the main owes both its birth and its growth to teaching" – We must acknowledge the fact that Education is transcendent, that the potential bound up within ourselves is undoubtedly impacted by the degree to which Education justly influences our Knowledge, and our Character and our Experience and our Condition.

Irrespective of how difficult it is to comprehend the consequential depths of angst and achievement and Virtue and Vice and progress and despair and Sovereignty and Hope, We must recognize the unique importance of Education within our lives and the lives of future generations.

More specifically, unless We wish to elevate Ignorance, a state of unknowing naturally at odds with an adept ability to choose, We must not turn our backs on these enlightened words of President Madison:

What spectacle can be more edifying or more seasonable, than that of Liberty & Learning, each leaning on the other for their mutual & surest support?[70]

Truth is – Our sages understood the relationship between "Liberty & Learning," between Education and "Thought, and Choice, and Power". They knew there is always a degree of exactness therein, regardless of how muddied our waters are.

Even when the scores of links connecting Education, Intellectual Virtue, and Liberty are indistinctively blurred and sure to foster our biased leans toward crude questions of Either-Or, our sages knew that so long as We possessed our abilities of Thought We would also have our abilities of Reason. They believed

We would be capable of fulfilling the full breadth of our responsibilities.

And so it is that We should not be surprised to find our subject of Education as the place where We must launch our new exertions.

Suppose we do genuinely value our ability to think and choose wisely. In such a case, would We not be eager to materialize our ability to graduate beyond a general appreciation of Lincoln's sentiment that "[education is] the most important subject which we as a people can be engaged in"? Would We not be more than willing to manifest his "desire to see the time when education, and by its means, morality, sobriety, enterprise and industry, shall become much more general than at present"?

We should be ready to embrace the relationship between Education and Power.

Furthermore, having already established the critical standing of "work worth doing" within our Political Economy, and believing We must surely value the importance of "[being able] to read" as illuminated by Lincoln, let us shine the bright lights of our ability to think and choose upon our arrangement of Free Enterprise and Representative Government.

Let us pivot from Education's role within the metaphysical vastness of Liberty to its importance inside our Corridors of Opportunity. Time it is to train our thoughts upon Lincoln's term "enterprise and industry" as it relates to these words of one of our more business-minded Presidents, William McKinley:

*Our future progress and prosperity depend upon
our ability to equal, if not surpass, other nations
in the enlargement and advance of science,
industry, and commerce.*[71]

Now, believing few of us unsettled by McKinley connecting "our future progress and prosperity" to "our ability to equal, if not surpass, other nations…", there ought not to be many willing to argue against Education's role in "[our] enlargement and advance of science, industry, and commerce."

There ought not to be many looking to discount the value of Education relative to the opportunities that naturally come along with "progress and prosperity". After all, considering Economy's definition as the productive management of the resources of a group of people – never mind, for a moment, issues surrounding the distribution of wealth – what exactly would the words "progress and prosperity" mean if Opportunity for the majority is scant? How do people – individuals and collections thereof – progress and prosper as the opportunities available to them are drying up?

There should be little doubt that We have exhibited a penchant for the misalignment of our priorities, but are We really to accept a reality wherein graduated opportunities are disconnected from "progress and prosperity"?

Are We uninterested in establishing clear links between Knowledge and Opportunity?

Are We up to the task of creating some graduated degree of a virtuous cycle between Education, Progress, and Prosperity?

So, with our attention turned to "enterprise and industry" and "work worth doing", and having previously touched upon the perverse theory declaring that We can thrive as a robust Nation of service providers and consumers pulled down the path to prosperity by low taxes, corporations, and the extraordinarily wealthy the world over, We need again look to *The Wealth of Nations*. We need to familiarize ourselves with the measure of our abilities as explained by Adam Smith:

> *...of the acquired and useful abilities of all the inhabitants and members of the society. The acquisition of such talents, by the maintenance of the acquirer during his education, study, or apprenticeship, always costs a real expense, which is a capital fixed and realized, as it were, in his person. Those talents, as they make a part of his fortune, so do they likewise that of the society to which he belongs.*[72]

It is the fact of this matter that somewhere along our way We as a people began to depredate what has become known as our Human Capital – our "capital fixed and realized". We lost sight of the importance of Education, not to mention Time and Experience, and We willfully ignored the reality that every pupil is a very real component of our society.

Somewhere along our way, We chose to stand still as Thought was corrupted and Choice degraded. We allowed Human Capital to be an asset intended for but a few, the tiny percentage of those amongst us determined to accumulate all the wealth that our Nation has to offer.

Somewhere along our way – while trying to elevate Greed to goodness, while watching as the economic expansion of our country was disconnected from the opportunities available to most of us – We became so distracted that We neglected the importance of our own Human Capital. Too many of us became willing to act as if our brains were not meant to be used beyond that required for hunting, gathering, or some other day long past.

Time it is for us to open our eyes to the ramifications of being, by and large, a society of evermore vulnerable service providers and consumers. Time it is to acknowledge the differences between the types of Labor and the relationship of each to "progress and prosperity" – to educate ourselves regarding the virtuous and the vicious economic realities of our work.

We the People, individually and collectively, must realize how our Condition is connected to what Adam Smith labeled the works of "productive and unproductive hands".

Please consider this abridged look at Smith's "Of the Accumulation of Capital, or of Productive and Unproductive Labour":

There is one sort of labour which adds to the value of the subject upon which it is bestowed; there is another which has no such effect. The former as it produces a value, may be called productive, the latter, unproductive... The labour of the latter, however, has its value, and deserves its reward as well as that of the former. But the labour of the manufacturer fixes and realizes itself in some particular subject or vendible commodity, which lasts for some time at least after that labour is past...

The labour of some of the most respectable orders in the society is, like that of menial servants, unproductive of any value... The sovereign, for example, with all the officers both of justice and war who serve under him, the whole army and navy, are unproductive labourers. They are the servants of the public, and are maintained by a part of the annual produce of the industry of other people. Their service, how honourable, how useful, or how necessary soever, produces nothing for which an equal quantity of service can afterwards be procured... In the same class must be ranked, some both of the gravest and most important, and some of the most frivolous professions; churchmen, lawyers, physicians, men of letters of all kinds; players, buffoons, musicians, opera-singers, opera-dancers, etc... Like the declamation of the actor, the harangue

*of the orator, or the tune of the musician, the
work of all of them perishes in the very instant of
its production.*[73]

To be brief, Time and Experience implore us to prioritize our efforts around McKinley's "enlargement and advance of science [and] industry", the economic conditions linked to "productive" Labor.

We cannot be confused regarding this, for to rearrange McKinley's list is to place "commerce" atop "the manufacturer" – it is to either equate or subordinate Smith's "productive" Labor to "unproductive" Labor and to entrench the Monied Interests along with their schemes of Pyramid – it is to encourage, if not legitimize, the work of Ponzi. This, by now, We should know.

We should by now be prepared to rightly value the productive nature of science and industry as opposed to that of commerce, and We should be able to connect Education to our priorities.

Moreover, regarding the folded truths of Education, Human Capital, Labor, Progress, and Condition, We should realize that technology has blurred our vision.

Captain, listen and know that We can no longer afford to consent to schemes of Education undertaken pursuant unto themselves. The moment has come for you to lead, for you to communicate to every man, woman, and child the purpose of learning: Our perpetual need to better process information in order to justly exert the Power emanating from our Unalienable Right of Thought and Choice.

We must begin to connect Education to our goal of being more in control of our own lives, including being able to graduate one's Opportunity if one so chooses. Here begins our path to "progress and prosperity," the base of Virtue's Happiness, and the just defense of our treasured Free Will.

As to our "methods of teaching and learning in schools" – be it either from the vantage of "progress and prosperity" or the formula of Liberty itself – it is quite remarkable that We have allowed our primary and secondary public schools, our most fundamental structures of Education, to develop into a national pastime.

We have tolerated a carousel of political calculations and the edicts thereof. We have effectually questioned the governmental involvement in the development of our Nation, and for good measure, our empty efforts have provided a near-perfect illustration of our reluctance and or our inability to hold the entrusted to account for the ineptitude of their works.

Hence, while acknowledging that a good Education goes well beyond our need for primary and secondary schools, and too knowing that We will, at worst, be marked audaciously naïve by the various Creatures of Control and the Status Quo, let us present a summarized plan for how We might effectively diffuse Knowledge throughout our public schools. No, We are not so presumptuous as "to dictate any plan or system". Our objective is to illustrate how the energy of Education can be linked to the mechanics of Opportunity vis-à-vis the utilization of Liberty's elements.

Our respectful ambition is to see the day when our Nation is worthy of these words left for us by an aging President Madison:

I congratulate you on the foundation thus laid for a general System of Education, and hope it presages a superstructure, worthy of the patriotic forecast which has commenced the Work. The best service that can be rendered to a Country, next to that of giving it liberty, is in diffusing the mental improvement equally essential to the preservation, and the enjoyment of the blessing.[74]

We must begin to show the entrusted that, in a tangible sense, a "superstructure" capable of fostering the symbiotic relationship between Education and Opportunity can be designed. We must demand "a general System of Education" that connects our public and private interests of Opportunity to our elements of Knowledge, Character, Experience, and Condition. We intend to "think anew, and act anew."

Sad to say, but if our Captain were courageously motivated, We would have crafted a way out of our dilemma long ago. We would have already tied together our arrangements of Education and Opportunity. Nevertheless, and despite the ineptitude to date, few of our collective concerns are as compatible with the arrangements of our Republic as that of Education – with the States and their districts able to function as independent laboratories within a competitive array designed to find solutions to an exigency as varied in detail as are the localities of our Nation.

Captain, the day has come for our Nation to construct a set of irresistible incentives for business entities to invest in Education. Instead of employing federal authority as dictator of policy, the day has come for you to stand aside and but guide a process built around locally controlled bodies charged with cultivating our national human resources while strengthening the ties that bind us. Time it is for you to lay "the foundation" upon which our many States and their school districts can go to work – each more than willing and able to function as incubators of their own ways and ideas. Time it is for you to personify this statement of President Franklin Roosevelt:

> *The country needs and, unless I mistake its temper, the country demands bold, persistent experimentation. It is common sense to take a method and try it: If it fails, admit it frankly and try another. But above all, try something. The millions who are in want will not stand by silently forever while the things to satisfy their needs are within easy reach.*[75]

Before listing the enterprise incentives central to our course of action, We propose that local mechanisms of regulation – Education Councils, if We may – be charged with first identifying the needs of local schools and then matching those needs with available assets as bid by the business community. In other words, Education Councils – uniformly comprised of selected school board members, teachers, parents, local business leaders, and government officials – would identify specific deficiencies within the local school system and then list those needs. Business enterprises would then compete for the right to invest in schools by bidding assets appropriate to a specific deficiency on the listings, with local councils selecting bids based on the relative qualifications of the assets.

Thus, local interests are entrusted with identifying the needs of their schools and then coordinating the available assets of businesses to meet those needs.

While our strategy stresses the involvement of the local business community, bids for education investments ought to be wider than local enterprises, for such a limitation would be impractical and unwarranted. In fact, seeing as Education Councils would be organized by the individual States, and assuming businesses would refrain from nonsensical investing, our plan will foster competition between localities and States alike.

The idea is to allow our laboratories within the States to compete in a national effort to find suitable remedies for our shared problem.

Concerning our deficiencies, private sector bids would be in the form of appropriate assets, with financial and non-financial assets (e.g. specialized instruction, construction labor, equipment, materials, transportation vehicles, facilities, etc.) qualifying for deficiency listings. The valuation of non-financial assets would logically be on a fair-market basis and be stipulated in the deficiency listings. Consequently, the acceptance of non-financial bids would be based on something other than a traditional least-cost method. A combination of best fit and least cost would logically apply.

Regarding our enterprise incentives, before We can enumerate, We the People must first agree to reset our tax structure. We must incentivize behaviors fostering our Human Capital.

We must agree that low taxes – especially those related to the Monied Interests and the Masters of Supply – have proven insufficient fuel for our "progress and prosperity". We must choose to utilize our ability to motivate via the use of targeted credits and cuts.

That is, while "not presuming" an appropriate standard level of taxation, the day has come for us to force our Captain to reverse many past tax reductions and encourage real investments in Education via targeted tax incentives.

The following incentives are proposed:

(1) substantial tax credits intended to reimburse contributing companies in part

(2) graduated long-term capital gains tax cuts for investors in contributing companies

(3) Targeted Education-Venture Area (TEVA) designations offering graduated versions of the first two incentives

Our first enumerated incentive begins the process of elevating Public Education to its proper place – atop our investments in Human Capital. Though not so presumptuous as to stipulate levels of credits, it is easy to foresee the invigorating effect of this. We trust that our Captain will not shy away from aggressive action. At the same time, and in addition to clearly recognizing the potential for manipulative abuse, the federal funds within the entirety of our plan must be used to supplement, not replace, State and local education funds.

Therefore, upon the budgetary establishment of the total amount of federal funding available to the whole of the States, our methodology for determining the amount of monies available to each State is the proverbial Tax Capacity[xi] of each State relative to their number of students, with each locality being a natural extension of this methodology. And, yes, seeing as this process of guiding the flow of supplemental funds is designed to ensure that our resources are invested fairly and efficiently, it is certainly possible that the market will leave many localities high and dry until they modify their ways. If no business is willing to fund a locality's stated priorities, then available monies would not be put to work.

Our second incentive calls for cutting the capital gains tax rate on long-term stock investments in

---

xi "Understanding Measures of Tax Effort and Tax Capacity." *William Penn Foundation*, 12 Apr. 2018, williampennfoundation. org/what-we-are-learning/understanding-measures-tax-effort-and-tax-capacity.

corporations that invest in our schools, with the amount of each cut tied directly to the level of Public Education investment, the Education Index (EI), on the part of each corporation.

As a result, the more a company invests in our Education, the greater the capital gains tax cut for its shareholders. As to calculating each corporation's Education Index, EI would be derived by dividing a company's total investments by its taxable income, smoothed over several years.

The Department of Education, no longer concerned with dictums of one sort or another, would be charged with (a) enforcing the integrity of the process and (b) enabling the process by releasing a yearly report detailing the Education Index of all corporations trading common stock within our Nation. Hence, the Department of Education would facilitate investors being able to evaluate the tax implications of their investments.

Yes, the entrusted will have to address whether to include companies not offering common stock, but We trust they are up to this assignment.

The final incentive comes attached to our Targeted Education-Venture Areas (TEVAs) – geographic locations wherein We combine our stated objectives of Education with the Opportunity goals of severely distressed Enterprise Zones. Thus, the unabashed purpose of the Targeted Education-Venture Area is to entice business operations, specifically those willing to invest in Public Education, into the TEVA.

Corporate investments in TEVAs would be rewarded with a significant increase in our standard tax credits, justifiably to eighty percent or more of the investment, perhaps in full, as well as a substantial boost to the weight of the investment as used in calculating the Education Index of the enterprise.

Of course, to encourage the establishment of TEVA incentives, these provisions would have to be applied for an extended period after the initial designation.

As to you naysayers, do not patronize us with claims of intricacy or trouble. We all know that many a year has passed since Homo erectus managed to light a fire. It would be best if you also acknowledged that our academic achievement problem involves far more than a skills gap.

Truth is – We should be able to agree that the subject of schooling this day is equally concerned with the ramifications of Opportunity and the mere meaning of a corporation, a keen understanding of capital and combinations, the full implications of Demand, and the ties that bind us together. Predispositions and past allegiances aside, We must agree that the purpose of Education today is complex and that our "superstructure" must be up to the challenge, that it must address Virtue and Vice and the many synapses of Power.

We the People are ready for action. And We should be able to agree that the day has come for our Federal Government to accept its role as conduit and catalyst – nothing more, nothing less.

Besides, does our plan not aggressively seek solutions to the multitude of our inadequacies while both expanding our Corridors of Opportunity and strengthening the ties that bind us? Have We not proposed solid incentives for corporations to invest in our Human Capital, the literal abilities of our Nation? Are We not encouraging market mechanisms to stoke our Liberty? And will not The Record see that We embraced the transcendent nature of Education – that We have labored to improve not only our Knowledge, but also our Character, Experience, and Condition?

Are We not ready to progress?

Fact is, the Status Quo today demands that We better educate ourselves so that We may secure jobs at the top of a global hierarchy wherein most of the "productive" work within the pecking order is intended to reside inside countries with lower economic standards. But the demands of our Status Quo – contrived for the sake of Corporate Profits and Concentrated Power – are little more than subversive gibberish, and We need not soothsayers to see the little pity that Time has prepared for us if We fail to change our ways.

In other words, We will eventually bring down our System if We do not successfully link Education to our Corridors of Opportunity and Liberty alike, if We continue to ignore these words of President Washington:

> *the best means of forming a [vigorous], virtuous and happy people, will be found in the right education of youth. Without this foundation,*

every other means, in my opinion, must fail; &
it gives me pleasure to find that [persons] of your
abilities are devoting their time & attention in
pointing out the way.[76]

To those of you finding President Washington's words regarding our "foundation" to be lacking, let us close our subject with this passage from his 1790 Annual Address to Congress:

...there is nothing which can better deserve
your patronage, than the promotion of Science
and Literature. Knowledge is in every country
the surest basis of publick happiness. In one, in
which the measures of government receive their
impression so immediately from the sense of the
community, as in our's, it is proportionately
essential. To the security of a free Constitution
it contributes in various ways: By convincing
those who are entrusted with the publick
administration, that every valuable end of
government is best answered by the enlightened
confidence of the people: And by teaching the
people themselves to know, and to value their own
rights; to discern and provide against invasions
of them; to distinguish between oppression
and the necessary exercise of lawful authority;
between burthens proceeding from a disregard to
their convenience, and those resulting from the
inevitable exigencies of society; to discriminate

> *the spirit of liberty from that of licentiousness, cherishing the first, avoiding the last, and uniting a speedy, but temperate vigilance against encroachments, with an inviolable respect to the laws.*[77]

XVII

Our Metaphysics

If a person only sees, or directs from day to day what is to be done, business can never go on methodically or well, for in case of sickness, or the absence of the Director, delays must follow. System in all things is the soul of business. To deliberate maturely, & execute promptly is the way to conduct it to advantage. With me, it has always been a maxim, rather to let my designs appear from my works, than by my expressions.[78]

– George Washington

Regarding the workings of our Political Economy – if We the People value our precepts of Care and Prudence, if We appreciate Duty and Virtue, if We recognize the rapport between Liberty and Reconciliation, if We can see our Demand and our Labor and our Scales of Justice together in the same light, and if We are willing to acknowledge the value of both the Division of Labor and Human Capital – then We should be prepared to advance a dispassionate discussion about what to do with our Liberty from this day forward. We should be ready to apply President Washington's words regarding "the soul of business" to the workings of our System.

Time it is for us to address President Adams' observation, "While all other Sciences have advanced, that of Government is at a Stand…".

More to the point, assuming We are willing to accept the universality of natural laws and the fact that We are not static – that We are a body in motion, "like a large fleet sailing under convoy" – let us show how the mechanisms of our metaphysical machine correspond, in a literal sense, to the structural interactions of advanced steam engines.[xii] Let us present a stable design for our propulsion process, one capable of withstanding the wayward ways of any Captain, and let us do so by applying the principles of thermodynamics – the branch of science that deals with the relationships between heat, work, temperature, and energy transfer. Let us show how our System was designed to convert our Free Will into energy and mechanical work by expanding our collected steam.

To begin, Liberty is our metaphysical working fluid. Our thoughts and our choices are the lifeblood of our Nation. Therefore, a mixture of our Knowledge,

---

xii Design akin to STaGE propulsion plant (Mitsubishi Heavy Industries)

our Character, our Condition, and our Experience is pumped into our boiler for conversion to superheated steam. This is plain and simple.

Regarding our pump, lest we risk becoming dead in the water, We must agree as to why and how We feed our Liberty into our Political Economy. We must all know that our fundamental mechanism – our essential Social Contract – is built around more or less the same set of metaphysical impellers free people have used throughout the ages when uniting with one another. And to be clear, the working fluid cannot enter the boiler without the pump.

We need to agree that our metaphysical pump is multistage, constructed upon the following trio of intrinsic desires, our most essential attachments of commonality:

(1) to defend property

(2) to practice religion or not

(3) to trade property

While the first two of our three impellers are noted in our Constitution, the third – to trade property – requires our examination. Although the defense of property and the practice of religion are somewhat straightforward, trading property is not, especially when valuing Labor as property. This is a critical point, for not only does the treatment of Labor often differentiate systems of

Political Economy, but those who cannot agree as to the whole of their reasoned need for one another will eventually conclude they have not that need.

Of course, if true to our cause, We must be willing to look beyond the principles of our Founders, to yet again Ancient Greece, specifically to Plato – Aristotle's predecessor. We must look to Plato's timeless Socratic dialogue, *The Republic*, wherein he established precedent for both the Division of Labor and Human Capital. It is there, near the outset of *The Republic*, an inquiry into no less a topic than justice and injustice, where We can begin to explore the weighty ramifications of one's comparative Right, or lack thereof, to Trade – to own and to gainfully sell, or lease or barter – one's own Labor.

We must turn to Plato's words related to "The barest notion of a State", submitted to The Record over 2,140 years before our Founders and Smith, and Marx, concerned themselves with the Division of Labor and the effects thereof:

> *And now let us see how our city will be able to supply this great demand: We may suppose that one man is a husbandman, another a builder, some one else a weaver – shall we add to them a shoemaker, or perhaps some other purveyor to our bodily wants?*

> *Quite right.*

The barest notion of a State must include four or five men.[79]

Here are the basics of our System.

Not to worry, a need to digress into an examination of *The Republic* is not at hand, but a closer inspection of our topic is required to understand our intrinsic desire to trade property as it connects to our purported dream of Opportunity. We must accept the inconveniences of our subject and dive deeper into *The Wealth of Nations*.

So – seeing as most any Reasonable Person would agree that *The Wealth of Nations* is a treatise on the wealth of nations, that Labor and Human Capital are related to our "work worth doing", and that We have already familiarized ourselves with Smith's delineation of Labor into Productive and Unproductive classifications – let us better acquaint ourselves with the Division of Labor as it is woven throughout The Record and into our Social Contract.

Fact is, these notions are not merely words. They are a fundamental part of our tangled reality – each is among the enduring characters within the passing stories of our lives, and it is our Duty to know them.

With our Social Contract in mind, please digest the following words of Smith, abridged to suit our conversation, and found under the headings "Of the Division of Labor" and "Of the Principle which gives Occasion to the Division of Labour:"

The greatest improvement in the productive powers of labour, and the greater part of the skill, dexterity, and judgment with which it is any where directed, or applied, seem to have been the effects of the division of labour.

This great increase in the quantity of work, which, in consequence of the division of labour, the same number of people are capable of performing, is owing to three different circumstances; first, to the increase of dexterity in every particular workman; secondly, to the saving of the time which is commonly lost in passing from one species of work to another; and, lastly, to the invention of a great number of machines which facilitate and abridge labour, and enable one man to do the work of many...

It is the great multiplication of the productions of all the different arts, in consequence of the division of labour, which occasions, in a well-governed society, that universal opulence which extends itself to the lowest ranks of the people. Every workman has a great quantity of his own work to dispose of beyond what he himself has occasion for; and every other workman being exactly in the same situation, he is enabled to exchange a great quantity of his own goods for a great quantity, or, what comes to the same thing, for the price of a great quantity of theirs.

He supplies them abundantly with what they have occasion for, and they accommodate him as amply with what he has occasion for, and a general plenty diffuses itself through all the different ranks of the society.[80]

This division of labour, from which so many advantages are derived, is not originally the effect of any human wisdom, which foresees and intends that general opulence to which it gives occasion. It is the necessary, though very slow and gradual, consequence of a certain propensity in human nature which has in view no such extensive utility; the propensity to truck, barter, and exchange one thing for another.

Whether this propensity be one of those original principles in human nature, of which no further account can be given; or whether, as seems more probable, it be the necessary consequence of the faculties of reason and speech, it belongs not to our present subject to enquire. It is common to all men, and to be found in no other race of animals, which seem to know neither this nor any other species of contracts...

As it is by treaty, by barter, and by purchase, that we obtain from one another the greater part of those mutual good offices which we stand in need of, so it is this same trucking disposition which originally gives occasion to the division of labour... And thus the certainty of being able to exchange all that surplus part of the produce of his own labour, which is over and above his own consumption, for such parts of the produce of other men's labour as he may have occasion for, encourages every man to apply himself to a particular occupation, and to cultivate and bring to perfection whatever talent or genius he may possess for that particular species of business...

Among men...the most dissimilar geniuses are of use to one another; the different produces of their respective talents, by the general disposition to truck, barter, and exchange, being brought, as it were, into a common stock, where every man may purchase whatever part of the produce of other men's talents he has occasion for.[81]

Obviously, We the People no longer live in 1776, and the pressures of Time have been equally applied to the marketplace and the idea of "every other workman being exactly in the same situation". Nonetheless, our "propensity to truck, barter, and exchange one thing for another" survives, as does our need to be honest with ourselves.

Is or is not Trade natural and the Division of Labor economical?

Is our pursuit of productivity not a part of our balancing act?

Can We not admit that "the skill, dexterity, and judgment" of Labor has in real terms taken a back seat to advances in material and information handling, macro and micro alike, not to mention artificial intelligence and the march of robotics – to technology and the masters thereof?

Is our society "well-governed", and do We truly value "work worth doing"?

What is the current state of Smith's "certainty" that "encourages every man to apply himself to a particular occupation", and do We of this day want President Washington's words regarding our "spirit of commerce" to still comprise a cornerstone of our collective being?

Furthermore, deeming a vast gulf of "situation" irrelevant is very unwise. Economic inequality is a prominent thread in Time – "situation" is the fiber upon which any Political Economy can easily slide.

Whether any one of us likes it or not, the gainful trading of one's own Labor is amongst our most basic of purposed bindings – it is a vital part of our ideals concerning Liberty and Justice for All – and if We cannot come to terms with this eternal truth, if We are willing to separate the Labor of an individual from the Condition of that individual, if We are willing to baptize corporations, never mind Happiness, then woe is already upon us.

Our Social Contract, our reasoned need for one another, is guaranteed to fail if We do not accept the progressed ramifications of Adam Smith's following words:

The property which every man has in his own labour, as it is the original foundation of all other property, so it is the most sacred and inviolable. The patrimony of a poor man lies in the strength and dexterity of his hands; and to hinder him from employing this strength and dexterity in what manner he thinks proper, without injury to his neighbour, is a plain violation of this most sacred property. It is a manifest encroachment upon the just liberty, both of the workman, and of those who might be disposed to employ him. As it hinders the one from working at what he thinks proper, so it hinders the others from employing whom they think proper.[82]

Now then, with Liberty as our working fluid and our Social Contract in mind, let us address the issue of how to both construct and provide for the workings of our metaphysical boiler. We must now address our heat source and the tubes within the boiler itself.

Regarding our heat source, this apparatus is comprised of duties delegated to our collective Captain. Hence, those We entrust are charged with setting a combustible blend of our joint aspiration and financial capital ablaze. Our Captain must both bring together and ignite a requisite combination of oxygen and fuel – which is no easy task because We are, in effect, expecting the entrusted to stoke our right fire while maneuvering our vessels and plotting a good course.

We expect those We entrust to proficiently function as a single skipper while performing the duties of the helmsman and watch engineer both personally and as one. No wonder We must be wise when choosing the entrusted.

Regarding the metaphysical tubes within our boiler, seeing as what exits our boiler is the steam of super-heated Liberty – our permutable factors of Knowledge and Character and Condition and Experience – our objective must be to develop our capabilities per Smith's words concerning "those talents, as they make a part of his fortune, so do they likewise that of the society to which he belongs." Unless we intend to be an incapable people of mottled means or a nation of warmongers or a peculiar blend of both – subjects of some sort – We must carefully construct our tubes using the principles of Human Capital.

Fortunately, if We will only entrust those eager to advance our priorities instead of the desires of those few finding themselves oh so Special, then this task should not be difficult. Have We not already herein presented a proposal for invigorating our contextual endeavor of learning?

At the very least, We should be able to expect sufficient appropriations for:

(1) sturdy supports for our families, since the elements of Thought and of Choice are borne and nurtured therein

(2) the persistent promotion of early childhood development, for a structure can only be as strong as the foundation upon which it rests

(3) the sparing of no efficient expense within the areas of primary and secondary education, for essential understanding will never come without a price

(4) assurances that our young adults will have easy and affordable access to university and technical instruction, for these are the men and women to carry the future

(5) investments in the absolute requirement of continuing education for our working men and women, because our society can ill afford to regularly kick aside a portion of its citizens if neither Marx nor some arrangement of bundled rods tied around an axe is to be of inspiration

(6) universally inexpensive options for the preservation of our good physical and mental health, for sound mind and body will always be the utmost importance of human necessities

(7) a commitment to construct a capable subsystem of rehabilitative corrections, for far too burdensome is the alternative

Our efforts will always be flawed. Our boiler will have exhausted waste – economized if its tubes are properly arranged – "But above all, try something" must be the adage of those We entrust if We are to press on as a people with the torch of Free Will secured in our grasp, held high for all to see.

Regarding our metaphysical throttle body – the mechanism through which Liberty is regulated per the requirements of reliable operations – this is yet another task for the entrusted. It is here where our Captain must contrive and apply our rules of commerce, combinations, workplace, environment, Trade, and Money and Banking, amongst others. And though it might be pleasant to suppose no such regulatory device is necessary, to go as fast as is possible forever, We, the People, cannot ignore either physics, physiology, or the insatiable appetites of a few.

Rules and regulations are an absolute requirement of any civil society, as President Washington here stated:

> for there never was a law yet made, I conceive, that hit the taste exactly of every man, or every part of the community. of course, if this be a reason for opposition, no law can be executed at all without force; & every man or set of men will, in that case, cut & carve for themselves. The consequences of which must be depricated by every class of men who are friends to order, & to the peace & happiness of the country.[83]

Unless We aspire to live in a reality wherein "every man or set of men will… cut & carve for themselves," it is natural and right for us to place justly regulated controls upon those interested in subduing our political or economic Liberty. Accordingly, let us herein propose three rudimentary improvements to our regulatory structure.

First, let us agree that no law or regulation should be enacted that We are not prepared to enforce vigorously. Let us also agree to repeal any law or regulation We are not ready to enforce. Just ask the owner of any small business in compliance what it is like to contend in the marketplace against competitors who disregard our laws and regulations because they know that enforcement is anything but likely. Too often, those disposed to operate outside of our rules enjoy a competitive advantage unavailable to citizens of higher repute. Law-abiding citizens are effectually penalized when enforcement is deficient.

There is right and there is wrong, and our lines of demarcation, at home and abroad, must be clear.

Second, to reflect our global reality, natural as rational Trade is, let us commit ourselves to use contemporary markers of manufacture – those used to indicate the locale of creation for any good or service – and let us not accept excuses of difficulty related to piecemeal manufacture and or scattered assembly. A considerable number of years have passed since We managed to split the atom, it has been many a day since We first sent people into Space, and We of this moment are more than accustomed to various labels and codes of all sorts. By now, the entrusted should be able to produce a simple arrangement of demarcation for our products, services, and shelves so that We may effortlessly mull over the ramifications of a potential purchase. And, yes, We propose this course of action in place of antagonistic tariffs and the like. Let Liberty work.

We must embody these words of Smith, again found within the pages of *The Wealth of Nations*:

> *As every individual, therefore, endeavours as much as he can both to employ his capital in the support of domestic industry, and so to direct that industry that its produce may be of the greatest value; every individual necessarily labours to render the annual revenue of the society as great as he can. He generally, indeed, neither intends to promote the public interest, nor knows how much he is promoting it...*[84]

Regarding our third improvement to our metaphysical throttle body, so that We can further contemplate putting our assets to work "in the support of domestic industry", let us require each entity conducting business in our United States – for profit or otherwise – to furnish us with a regular summary of its ownership, expressly in terms of the percentages held by persons and or entities of each nationality, derived if necessary.

Considering the incessant mining of our personal data as individual customers and prospects in this very commercial world of ours, as well as the depth of thought that went into creating credit default swaps and other ostensible instruments of high finance, neither this nor our other regulatory improvements should be too much to ask.

You prefer to do business with upstanding fellow citizens, do you not?

Remember, our System was meant for a people "possessed of the spirit of commerce". Our Political Economy was structured in such a way as to promote an American Dream – a simple desire to have "the chance to work hard at work worth doing" – and if We want this intention of our sages to hold today, then our regulations must reflect our natural "disposition to truck, barter, and exchange".

Next, upon passing through our throttle body, our superheated Liberty turns three metaphysical Turbines of Endeavour. And though our engine is metaphysical, these turbines are very real – ordered first to improve our capital stocks, then our services of facilitation and comfort, and lastly, our common needs existing outside the realm of profit. We should by now be able to understand this construct as handed down through the years, for it is in this combination of commonality where Opportunity has always resided.

Below is a synopsis of how our Liberty is, sequentially, put to work inside the market:

(1) Our initial turbine, through which our
metaphysical steam rapidly expands, is our

High-Pressure Turbine of Production. It is here, amongst blades constructed of both extraction and manufacturing, where Smith's Productive opportunities abound.

(2) Once through our most fundamental endeavors, our abilities are channeled towards our secondary boiler to be reheated by our physical infrastructure. Yes, our construct depends upon adequate appropriations for our physical infrastructure – the responsibility of Government at every level.

(3) Once reheated, our metaphysical steam then enters and expands through our Intermediate Pressure Turbine of Private Services – our increasingly large blades of modern necessity and nicety, including those of transportation, information, the balance of skilled trades, entertainment, and our many financial and personal services – the vast majority of which involve Unproductive opportunities.

(4) Our third turbine is our Low-Pressure Turbine of Public Services – non-profit, governmental, and military entities – the opportunities of which are Unproductive.

(5) Finally, upon passing through our three turbines, our permutable factors are condensed for

recirculation back to our boiler and our more graduated questions of Human Capital.

Therefore, our metaphysical turbine shafts are connected to our three turbines, each independently turned by the opportunities within each turbine. These shafts, Turbine Shafts of Labor, are then brought together by a coordinated reduction inside a complex gearbox – our metaphysical Gearbox of Demand, the means by which our prop shaft and propeller are turned within our surroundings. And as one should expect, our gearbox's purpose is to convert the product of the torque and the rotational speed conveyed by our Labor into usable Power.

All of this is to say that Opportunity, Labor, and Demand are inextricably related and interdependent, and no person should be surprised that these components play such a critical role in the workings of our lives.

Even those economies with differing degrees of rearranged priorities have the same basic construct: Turbines of Endeavor, a Gearbox of Demand, and the Shafts of Labor connecting the two. Likewise, no matter where trouble originates – either with a misaligned or broken turbine shaft, a damaged turbine, or a gearbox that has seized up – any engine will eventually fail if its components are not adequately coordinated and maintained.

Such is the reality of the marketplace.

Now, having illuminated the essentials of our Political Economy – Opportunity and Labor and Demand, along with our governmental components – let us turn to the lubricant of our marketplace. Let us focus on Money and its Supply, along with this wisdom of Adams as he penned in one of his 1787 letters to Jefferson:

All the Perplexities, Confusions and Distresses in America arise not from defects in their Constitutions or Confederation, not from a want of Honour or Virtue, So much as from downright Ignorance of the Nature of Coin, Credit and Circulation.[85]

While it is reasonable to suspect that if President Adams were here today, he would update his position regarding "Honour [and] Virtue," he would no doubt reiterate his words concerning our "downright Ignorance of the nature of Coin, Credit and Circulation." He would be aghast by what We have done with our Money Supply. Truth is – As a whole, We are ignorant about our metaphysical lube oil, the stuff used to lubricate our all-important economic Gearbox of Demand.

Did or did We not stand still as our currency was separated from a firm basis of reality, as in pretty metals or seashells or feathers or the like?

Do or do We not now allow our Captain to manage our collective finances like a drunken sailor in possession of some fantastical device, a gadget used to plate paper so that it is both exportable and pliable per the desires of a few?

And have We not acted as if these decisions are of little to no consequence so long as We can stay sufficiently distracted, at least entertained, while trying to purchase ourselves to contentment?

But let us not digress.

What We must know is that our Money Supply is, today, a quasi-independent subsystem of our Political Economy, and – even though the pros and cons of our fiat currency and its management are debatable far beyond our scope herein – We must understand that the gearbox of our System is reliant upon a fluid and sound money, steadfast in every respect.

It is an absolute fact that if Demand is to reliably function at levels exponentially higher than the restraints of barter, not to mention the complexities of the day, then Money must be stable, employed, and secure. It took Adam Smith, in "Of the Accumulation of Capital, or of Productive and Unproductive Labour", but ten words to perfectly explain the purpose of our metaphysical lubricant:

The sole use of money is to circulate consumable goods.[86]

Again, our reality is not 1776, but if We are to better understand the evolved role of Money, We must begin to appreciate the genetic characteristics of Capital and Revenue and how each relates to production, consumption, Labor, and wealth. Only upon doing this – getting back to where We are willing to distinguish Capital from Revenue – can we rightly differentiate those in

Plato's "barest notion of a State" from the multitude of our service providers.

We must understand the differences between, and the ramifications of, Productive and Unproductive Labor. Hence, despite the boring aggravation, We need to continue our look into *The Wealth of Nations*.

With our notations interspersed, please digest these abridged words of Smith, as this wisdom is manifestly related to our Money, its Supply, and the weighty ramifications thereof:

> *Though the whole annual produce of the land and labour of every country is no doubt ultimately destined for supplying the consumption of its inhabitants, and for procuring a revenue to them... it naturally divides itself into two parts. One of them, and frequently the largest, is, in the first place, destined for replacing a capital, or for renewing the provisions, materials, and finished work, which had been withdrawn from a capital; the other for constituting a revenue either to the owner of this capital, as the profit of his stock, or to some other person, as the rent of his land. Thus, of the produce of land, one part replaces the capital of the farmer; the other pays his profit and the rent of the landlord; and thus constitutes a revenue both to the owner of this capital, as the profits of his stock, and to some other person as the rent of his land. Of the produce of a great manufactory, in the same manner, one part, and*

that always the largest, replaces the capital of the undertaker of the work; the other pays his profit, and thus constitutes a revenue to the owner of this capital.

That part of the annual produce of the land and labour of any country which replaces a capital, never is immediately employed to maintain any but productive hands. It pays the wages of productive labour only. That which is immediately destined for constituting a revenue, either as profit or as rent, may maintain indifferently either productive or unproductive hands.[87]

Is or is not Adam Smith the so-called "father of capitalism," and is there not sound reasoning in how he relates Capital to Productive Labor?

Can We not agree with Smith regarding Revenue (profit or rent) and his assertion that it "may maintain indifferently either productive or unproductive hands"?

Are our metaphysical turbines not logical?

Let Smith continue:

Whatever part of his stock a man employs as a capital, he always expects it to be replaced to him with a profit. He employs it, therefore, in maintaining productive hands only; and after having served in the function of a capital to him, it constitutes a revenue to them. Whenever he employs any part of it in maintaining unproductive hands of any kind, that part is from that moment withdrawn from his capital, and placed in his stock reserved for immediate consumption.[88]

Yes, one person's Revenue can be construed as another person's Capital, but does not the exponential growth of such logic corrupt its foundation?

Have We not conflated Smith's underpinnings of Capital and Revenue, and have We not reimagined the word "stock" while allowing schemes of Pyramid and Ponzi to ascend?

Can We not understand the folly of trying to be a healthy Nation of service providers and consumers pulled down the path to prosperity by low taxes, corporations, and the extraordinarily wealthy the world over?

Again, *The Wealth of Nations* is dated 1776. Have Greed and self-indulgence gotten the best of us?

Let Smith continue:

Unproductive labourers, and those who do not labour at all, are all maintained by revenue... The rent of land and the profits of stock are everywhere, therefore, the principal sources from which unproductive hands derive their subsistence. These are the two sorts of revenue of which the owners have generally most to spare. They might both maintain indifferently, either productive or unproductive hands. They seem, however, to have some predilection for the latter. The expense of a great lord feeds generally more idle than industrious people. The rich merchant, though with his capital he maintains industrious people only, yet by his expense, that is, by the employment of his revenue, he feeds commonly the very same sort as the great lord.

The proportion, therefore, between the productive and unproductive hands, depends very much in every country upon the proportion between that part of the annual produce, which, as soon as it comes either from the ground, or from the hands of the productive labourers, is destined for replacing a capital, and that which is destined for constituting a revenue, either as rent or as profit. This proportion is very different in rich from what it is in poor countries.[89]

Is this not the practicalities of our Economy, and who amongst us would like to disagree with either the preeminent importance of production or Smith's titling of *The Wealth of Nations*?

Can We not understand why markets for shares in corporations have become altogether detached from our reality, that of the People?

We need to continue with Smith's words:

That part of the annual produce, therefore, which, as soon as it comes either from the ground, or from the hands of the productive labourers, is destined for replacing a capital, is not only much greater in rich than in poor countries, but bears a much greater proportion to that which is immediately destined for constituting a revenue either as rent or as profit. The funds destined for the maintenance of productive labour are not only much greater in the former than in the latter, but bear a much greater proportion to those which, though they may be employed to maintain either productive or unproductive hands, have generally a predilection for the latter.

The proportion between those different funds necessarily determines in every country the general character of the inhabitants as to industry or idleness... Our ancestors were idle for want of a sufficient encouragement to industry. It is better, says the proverb, to play for nothing than to work for nothing... The idleness of the greater part of the people who are maintained by the expense of revenue, corrupts, it is probable, the industry of those who ought to be maintained by the employment of capital, and renders it less advantageous to employ a capital there than in other places.[90]

And so it is that the permutable factors of Liberty come into the light. Can We not see how the structural interactions of our Political Economy impact our Knowledge, Character, Experience, and Condition?

Maybe these next words of Smith will help those still lagging:

> *The proportion between capital and revenue, therefore, seems every-where to regulate the proportion between industry and idleness. Wherever capital predominates, industry prevails: wherever revenue, idleness. Every increase or diminution of capital, therefore, naturally tends to increase or diminish the real quantity of industry, the number of productive hands, and consequently the exchangeable value of the annual produce of the land and labour of the country, the real wealth and revenue of all its inhabitants...*

> *The annual produce of the land and labour of any nation can be increased in its value by no other means, but by increasing either the number of its productive labourers, or the productive powers of those labourers who had before been employed.*[91]

No disrespect to Unproductive Labor or those charged with our Money and its Supply, but We should all be able to agree that it is "the productive powers" of Productive Labor that determine "the real wealth" of a society. We should be able to understand how our persistent efforts to elevate Revenue to a level at or above that of Capital are extraordinarily unwise. Can We not be honest with ourselves?

Have We not allowed Revenue to reign, and do We not collectively worship a bull?

Self-righteous indignation aside, we should not be perplexed when told, "Our ancestors were idle for want of a sufficient encouragement to industry. It is better, says the proverb, to play for nothing than to work for nothing."

Know this – Any competent engineer will warn of the gearbox seizing if a buildup of filth is allowed to degrade the functional capacity of the lubricant. God forbid the lube oil mixes with the working fluid or flows into the boiler room.

Therefore, by utilizing rules and regulations, We must always mitigate the following:

(a) the immense wealth coagulating around Money itself, unless designs on paper are to be valued as production

(b) the ways and means of wild-eyed speculators in both equities and instruments, unless We are to be vulnerable to flights of the imagination

(c) the very idea of "too big to fail," unless We shall bow to these entities and their masters

(d) the exorbitant rewards associated with financial incentives of the short term, unless gamesmanship is to be accepted as our norm

(e) the tendency for currencies and economies to become uncontrollably entwined, unless We are to be citizens of this world instead of our Nation

(f) the many consequential manifestations of temperament sure to be regretted, unless "the love of soft living and the get-rich-quick theory of life" shall be an admired state

Finally, while acknowledging the omission of a few ancillary parts and pieces, our metaphysical engine would only be complete if We included our need to inject additional working fluid into our System. That is, a subsystem of managed immigration is necessary, for just as our boiler will have exhausted waste, there will surely be days when our System requires an infusion of working fluid.

Whether or not you wish to admit it, an addition of those deprived of their Liberty is often needed, per our Lady:

Not like the brazen giant of Greek fame,
With conquering limbs astride from land to land;
Here at our sea-washed, sunset gates shall stand
A mighty woman with a torch, whose flame

Is the imprisoned lightning, and her name
Mother of Exiles. From her beacon-hand
Glows world-wide welcome; her mild eyes command
The air-bridged harbor that twin cities frame.
"Keep, ancient lands, your storied pomp!" cries she
With silent lips. "Give me your tired, your poor,
Your huddled masses yearning to breathe free,
The wretched refuse of your teeming shore.
Send these, the homeless, tempest-tost to me,
I lift my lamp beside the golden door!"[92]

But why does this metaphysical exercise matter?

In short, while uncertainty is a fact of being, We can be sure of Power's reality. Not all Power is of the same ilk – there is that which is good and that which is not. Hence, whatever the amount of force associated with one's Power, or what one decides to do with that Power, We can ill afford to be blind to the implications of Power's disposition.

Our metaphysics matters because our Power is far more than our physical might and because Virtue and Vice are the harbingers of Thought and Choice.

Our metaphysics matters because our Power represents the very nature of our mental and moral efficacy.

In other words, our approach to reality and being – the evidence of how We choose to process all that exists, including that which is well beyond our horizon – is the definitive testimony of our lives. Whatever our size or strength, our metaphysics matters because We determine the sort of Power We generate.

Our sages knew this – they knew that irrespective of the force We possess or the words We profess, it is how We use the sole Unalienable Right of Liberty that matters. Yes, they fell far short during their day, as will We, but they created the blueprint humankind needed to progress. They gave us the guidance required to justly bind together "Thought, and Choice, and Power".

Regardless of the leeway some think We deserve; our metaphysics matters because our System matters.

Our metaphysics matters, now more than ever, because with the accumulated "wisdom of our sages and blood of our heroes" at our disposal, We have been afforded more than enough Time to get it right. Our metaphysics matters because the day has come for us – We the People – to fulfill our Duty to oppose the extremes.

Time it is to follow the narrow path, the metaphysical middle point where Care and Prudence meet, the path towards "a more perfect Union".

XVIII

In Response

in every country where man is free to think & to speak, differences of opinion will arise from difference of perception, & the imperfection of reason. but these differences, when permitted, as in this happy country, to purify themselves by free discussion, are but as passing clouds overshadowing our land transiently, & leaving our horizon more bright & serene.[93]

— Thomas Jefferson

Seeing as some are so rooted in their perceptions and their reasons that they will ardently oppose the idea of a narrow path, irrespective of its reckoning, do allow us a few final words and considerations.

Is our Political Economy not, in fact, John Adams' "large fleet sailing under convoy," and do you not think our intended heading is one wherein our System operates on behalf of the People?

Are We wrong to believe that George Washington's words concerning "the spirit of commerce" belong within our definition of Allegiance, and are common goals not an indispensable part of our Sovereignty?

Is there not truth within Franklin Roosevelt's belief "that government is ourselves and not an alien power over us"?

Is it, or is it not, our collective responsibility to follow Abraham Lincoln's instruction to "think anew, and act anew"?

And why do some of you act as if Virtue is irrelevant and our Labor unworthy of protection?

How can anyone contest the metaphysical importance of our System?

We should differentiate those still resistant to our narrow path. Indeed. So, let us now separate what We, the Reasonable People, have to say to those of you far to our left and those of you far to our right.

First, let us respond to those who believe that Economy does not transcend Government – those of you to the left who look for Government to have greater command.

In the starkest of terms, you may suppose self-styled Communists, enthusiastic Socialists, and wild-eyed Capitalists, gung-ho Fascists too, worlds apart, but the truth is that each is out to advance their version of control. They each find Jefferson's "rightful liberty" to be a nuisance. On balance, they are of the same ilk, they are related, because those out to command – Opportunity, or Knowledge, or morals or mores, or anything else – all possess a desire to discount humanity's responsibility of balancing one's Free Will against the "equal rights of others." Regardless of how differently they may be clothed, they all shrug at the constraints of Justice.

Truth is – Dub one another as We may, neither Greed nor Pride is interested in our labels, and We each reside along the same continuum of Virtue and Vice.

This is not to declare that anyone ought to ignore others borne in Time – for example, Karl Marx and his ideas – or that societies can endure fast-moving merry-go-rounds of morals and mores. On the contrary, stability is of vital importance in life, and if We are to guard against the conditions which are known to destabilize peoples, those which ripen societies for the rise of adversaries to Liberty and Justice, then We must familiarize ourselves with all points of view – Marx's included.

Likewise, has Time not already exposed the reasoning of Karl Marx to be not a matter of what should be done, but an illustration of the circumstances that We must resist?

To be more precise, seeing as We have already herein touched upon the historical importance of the Division of Labor and the reality of Human Capital, it behooves us to acknowledge the "Labour Power" of Marx, as he submitted to The Record in 1847 within his work titled *Wage Labour and Capital*:

> *We thus see how the method of production and the means of production are constantly enlarged, revolutionized, how division of labor necessarily draws after it greater division of labor, the employment of machinery greater employment of machinery, work upon a large scale work upon a still greater scale. This is the law that continually throws capitalist production out of its old ruts and compels capital to strain ever more the productive forces of labor for the very reason that it has already strained them – the law that grants it no respite, and constantly shouts in its ear: March! march! This is no other law than that which, within the periodical fluctuations of commerce, necessarily adjusts the price of a commodity to its cost of production.*[94]

These words of Marx, though some will avoid them no matter the consequence, are a superb explanation as to why We cannot afford to be Ignorant, for in a mere 125 words, he illustrates one of our greatest dangers: If some unknown plurality of us concludes that chants of "March! march!" has killed our dream of "work worth doing", then soon after that every single one of us will begin to comprehend the societal ramifications of having all of our scabs completely scraped off of our imperfections. And let us not be mistaken – the label We use for our new state will be inconsequential.

Hindsight being what it is, those in the future may determine that this state is already upon us.

This may be inconvenient, but those advocating for command come in many forms, and it is our responsibility to avoid the conditions that have proven to be their invitation – "to steer clear of the shelves & rocks [humankind has] struck upon".

President Grover Cleveland, in his 1888 State of the Union Address, adequately exposed this thread in Time:

> *Communism is a hateful thing and a menace to peace and organized government; but the communism of combined wealth and capital, the outgrowth of overweening cupidity and selfishness, which insidiously undermines the justice and integrity of free institutions, is not less dangerous than the communism of oppressed poverty and toil, which, exasperated by injustice and discontent, attacks with wild disorder the citadel of rule.*[95]

"…the communism of combined wealth and capital, the outgrowth of overweening cupidity and selfishness," these words provide a suitable segue for us to respond to those of you eager to push your own devilish brand of unfettered capitalism – those of you far to our right that always long to pimp Supply and neuter Government.

We can now see how quick you are to argue against Demand – to declare that you and your kind are responsible for pulling us and our Demand down the road to your dream.

We see how you constantly decry the regulatory effects of laws and how you scoff at the Justice within Theodore Roosevelt's "[no] crookedness in the dealing." And do not think We cannot recognize your desire to lower our safeguards to that of the wanting found elsewhere, as well as your belief that short-term incentives are superior to any moderating incentive otherwise. Your desire to consume everything in sight – including the Happiness of others – is now well-known.

As to your ghostly ways, in your effort to provide camouflage for modern-day money changers and their kith and kin – a clan of which you are – you have exploited the "invisible hand" of Adam Smith, a metaphorical device he employed barely a few times. But deceive as you do, We know all too well how you have managed to disconnect our Labor from our well-being, and We now realize how you have patronized us with words you so smugly suppose are perfect for us – for simpletons.

Yes, it is evident that you have used Smith's "invisible hand" to advance your brand of laissez-faire – your mission has been to remove as many societal restraints as possible. You wish to leave the Monied Interests to their own devices as they subjugate our Liberty of Demand and our Labor to their wants.

Decades ago, some of your ideas were – arguably – worth thrusting into action, but just as the words of our sages have been subjected to the pressures of Time, so too have your policies.

We can now see how your loving Supply – the offspring of conspicuous Capital and the sibling of monied favor – treats those willing to submit themselves, irrespective of geography. We can now see how your theories and words are a complete joke – how you mock the basics of our Pledge while you laugh at our notion of Happiness.

Your failed ideas, if not you, have proven to possess no need for Reconciliation or our narrow path. You have shown yourself uninterested in "leaving our horizon more bright & serene."

Know this – Though our convictions may compel us to tolerate your vain tendencies and wanderlust for your splendid chasm, We are in no way obligated to bow to your wishes. We are in no way obliged to embrace the Power of one or a few or many as that Power looks to command, if not feed upon, our Liberty.

We have grown tired of going along with your wayward ways and your exploitation of Freedoms and Rights at our expense.

Time it is for you to open your mind to Virtue – to rethink your lack of investment in Liberty and Justice, for All. Time it is for you to either change your ways – confessing your past deeds – or go to your gulch and stay there. We can manage just fine without you.

As for you of the entrusted so willing to subordinate us to those of corrupted mind, how lacking – at best – are you? And how does that look stay upon your face? How is it that you can celebrate as you degrade our Power? Never mind. All you need to know is that

We now understand why John Adams warned about the "abuse of Words" and how such tactics are "the great instrument of Sophistry and Chicanery – of party, faction and Division in Society". The day has come for you too to change your ways, for you to contemplate the evidence of your life as it increasingly correlates to these later words of Adams:

> *Remember Democracy never lasts long. It soon wastes exhausts and murders itself. There never was a Democracy Yet, that did not commit suicide. It is in vain to Say that Democracy is less vain, less proud, less selfish, less ambitious or less avaricious than Aristocracy or Monarchy. It is not true in Fact and no where appears in history. Those Passions are the same in all Men under all forms of Simple Government, and when unchecked, produce the same Effects of Fraud Violence and Cruelty. When clear Prospects are opened before Vanity, Pride, Avarice or Ambition, for their easy gratification, it is hard for the most considerate Phylosophers and the most conscientious Moralists to resist the temptation. Individuals have conquered themselves, Nations and large Bodies of Men, never.*[96]

To each of you entrusted with our ballasts of Government, listen as We say the plank is ready. You should not expect us, the Reasonable People, to stand still as our next wave of tumult builds in plain sight. We are awake, impatient, and expect you to go about – with much haste – correlating our efforts to ascending our personal "ease, comfort, security."

Time it is for you – no matter how you identify with us, and irrespective of your past objectives, your past indiscretions, your empty promises to date – to make amends and lead as We expect. Your day is upon you.

Aye, Captain, the day has come for you to ensure that our alienable banners of Freedoms and Rights are no longer used as cover for those wanting to self-righteously press their boots upon our necks. The day has come for those of you We have entrusted with our Government to reflect upon your duplicitous ways and your betrayals when you recite our Pledge:

> *I pledge allegiance to the Flag of the United States of America, and to the Republic for which it stands, one Nation under God, indivisible, with liberty and justice for all.*[97]

As to our Duty, that of the People, there can be absolutely no doubt that "with liberty and justice for all" has proven to be humanity's most bothersome thread – ours included – and that the two smallest words, "for all", have been particularly challenging.

Fact is, none of us should be surprised that the issues before us today revolve around the same circumstances our kind has encountered many a day before. Our exigencies yet again have to do with these sentences below, spoken over a century ago by President Wilson during his first inauguration:

> *Nor have we studied and perfected the means by which government may be put at the service of humanity, in safeguarding the health of the Nation, the health of its men and its women and its children, as well as their rights in the struggle for existence. This is no sentimental duty. The firm basis of government is justice, not pity. These are matters of justice. There can be no equality or opportunity, the first essential of justice in the body politic, if men and women and children be not shielded in their lives, their very vitality, from the consequences of great industrial and social processes which they can not alter, control, or singly cope with. Society must see to it that it does not itself crush or weaken or damage its own constituent parts. The first duty of law is to keep sound the society it serves. Sanitary laws, pure food laws, and laws determining conditions of labor which individuals are powerless to determine for themselves are intimate parts of the very business of justice and legal efficiency.*[98]

Wilson's own shortcomings aside – dogmatic customs being what they are – the problems of this advanced day still revolve around Justice and its role, as he so chronicled in 1913. The questions before us have to do with the fact that far too many, even now, find no problem with the People having to always include in their prayers a request that their families be "shielded… from the consequences of great industrial and social processes which they can not alter, control, or singly cope with."

The burning crux of our difficulties still revolves around those of you who believe it silly for anyone to think prayers better suited for matters of forgiveness and wisdom and gratitude – the righteous concerns of Free Will, of bad choices and good choices and lives well-lived.

Furthermore, how – in good conscience – can you guardians of Vice and you custodians of the Status Quo carry on as if our United States of America was designed to have a sizable portion of us fated to living lives of either subservient toil, unfulfilling dearth, or stagnant effect because you do not value the Virtue within one's uncomplicated desire to work hard?

From where is the reasoning behind the ruin of our ability to earn a good living – of far too many of us being frozen in Time, all but powerless to progress?

How does a Nation intended to be of the People move forward if the People themselves cannot earn both good and reliable income for their work – if We cannot better ourselves nor the prospects of our families?

Do you honestly think your strategies are of that which must be good, and are you prepared to testify as to which side you are on?

The evidence is clear – you have acted as if Justice is a theoretical nuisance. You have been busy trying to dismantle our American Dream.

Regarding the exact causes of why some of you are still compelled to scoff at the narrow path, the seed of your opinions might never be known to us. Be that as it may, the day has come for all of us to be the masters of our livelihoods within a healthy construct of Supply and Demand. We can settle on these words of Lincoln, spoken during the last of The Great Debates, with Stephen Douglas, to sufficiently illuminate your perceptions and your reasons:

> *That is the real issue. That is the issue that will continue in this country when these poor tongues of Judge Douglas and myself shall be silent. It is the eternal struggle between these two principles – right and wrong – throughout the world. They are the two principles that have stood face to face from the beginning of time, and will ever continue to struggle. The one is the common right of humanity and the other the divine right of kings. It is the same principle in whatever shape it develops itself. It is the same spirit that says, 'You work and toil and earn bread, and I'll eat it.' No matter in what shape it comes, whether from the mouth of a king who seeks to bestride the people of his own nation and live by the fruit of their labor, or from one race of men as an*

apology for enslaving another race, it is the same tyrannical principle.[99]

"It is the same principle in whatever shape it develops itself", but good can be garnered from these words: We can shape our strategy in opposition!

Specifically, if We will cherish our Unalienable Right of Thought and Choice, if We will agree as to the supremacy of Economy and the standing of "work worth doing", if We will value our Liberty of Demand, and if We will pursue the idea of Virtuous Cycles of Endeavor, then there is nothing keeping us from being able to set ourselves on a course that both strengthens our abilities related to work and sweetens the fruits of our natural want to Trade. Nothing is keeping us from recognizing that Demand is a product of our Liberty and that Supply falls squarely within the domain of the Monied Interests.

Apart from our willingness to shun Supply's intoxicating brew – their fermentation of easy access to cash, credit, and extraordinarily low prices, often some combination of each, with every batch formulated to distort our Demand with only a few swigs of the concoction – nothing is keeping us from exerting the Free Will that We are sanctioned with and thereby moving Supply in the direction of our collective choosing.

If We the People will dedicate ourselves to being wise directors of our Demand, along our way entrusting only those devoted to our cause, then righting our course is well within our capabilities.

And to you others elsewhere, please know that none of this is to say that We believe trading amongst nations to be wrong or undesirable. We so very simply desire to Trade goods and services rather than Labor. We believe in legitimate competition based on quality, efficiency, distinctiveness, and unadulterated value. We respect all structures of Political Economy built upon Liberty, and We believe in several things well-regulated – not the least of which is Capitalism. We consider all border-lines of demarcation to still be of meaning and value, and We know our moment is upon us. We, the Reasonable People of these United States, know that the day has come for us to end our compliance and amend the future. We hope you, too, are ready for the challenge.

We can correct the order of this world – and even though We cannot see into the entire continuum of Time, We should be thankful that We have not been relieved of our choices.

Time it is for our revolution – for us each to see that, in the end, our lives are defined by our choices and that some critical mass of us can set off a chain reaction of events destined to change the course We are currently on.

Time it is for us to appreciate these words written in 1815 by John Adams to his old friend and bitter rival, Thomas Jefferson:

As to the history of the Revolution, my Ideas may be peculiar, perhaps Singular. What do We mean by the Revolution? The War? That was no part of the Revolution. It was only an Effect and

Consequence of it. The Revolution was in the Minds of the People, and this was effected, from 1760 to 1775, in the course of fifteen Years before a drop of blood was drawn at Lexington.[100]

So, having passably explored our current situation, having explored the depths of Allegiance and Sovereignty, having exposed our Power and the critical importance of Knowledge, having humbly offered an outline as to how We might breathe life anew into our dormant energies of Education, and having presented a systematic blueprint for the mechanical workings of our System, Time it is for us to say again: Our aim is a Renaissance of Liberty throughout the whole of our society.

Our objective is a revival whereby the Unalienable Right of Free Will can flourish within a System constituted to impartially balance the forces borne of all its citizens' thoughts and choices.

And in making this declaration, we believe that We find ourselves in the excellent company of our finest Presidents – aligned with their wisdom and words. It is our belief that Abraham Lincoln, if here today, would echo his remarks at Gettysburg:

[Twelve score and eight years ago] our fathers brought forth on this continent, a new nation, conceived in Liberty, and dedicated to the proposition that all men are created equal.[101]

We believe that the moment has come for us, We the People, to once and for all decide if We shall live up to these words inscribed upon The Liberty Bell:

Proclaim LIBERTY Throughout all the Land unto all the Inhabitants thereof
Lev. XXV. v X.[102]

Conclusion
Destiny

The world will little note, nor long remember what we say here, but it can never forget what they did here. It is for us the living, rather, to be dedicated here to the unfinished work which they who fought here have thus far so nobly advanced. It is rather for us to be here dedicated to the great task remaining before us – that from these honored dead we take increased devotion to that cause for which they gave the last full measure of devotion – that we here highly resolve that these dead shall not have died in vain – that this nation, under God, shall have a new birth of freedom – and that government of the people, by the people, for the people, shall not perish from the earth.[103]

– Abraham Lincoln

We are not, today, faced with a crisis like that which confronted Abraham Lincoln. Nevertheless, and though The Record is sure to bury the details of our lives within its depths, our story will read like Lincoln's and all others – it will explain both our Dysfunction and how We chose to exercise our sole Unalienable Right of Free Will.

Moreover, Time itself will tell our story – a drama filled with antagonists and untamed tales of Either-Or, all hostile to the diminishing powers of an ever more intoxicated protagonist – it will tell of how We assailed Allegiance and how We were determined to dismantle our armada. Time will tell of how We allowed our Captain to weaponize the Status Quo – how even Reasonable People are vulnerable when they choose to drift within the tide of the times. Aye, Time will tell of how We the People were derelict in our Duty.

Time will not hold back. Our voyage will be underscored by how We of this day used our Free Will – how We degraded our principles and dishonored hard work – how, when faced with an increasingly complex and rapidly changing sea, We chose to enlist ourselves into legions of Blue and Red.

Make no mistake, Time will testify that We chose to worship at the altar of Vice, that We championed Greed and devalued Truthfulness, that We deserted Temperance, and that We stood still as Care and Prudence were stripped of meaning.

Time will testify that We collectively turned our backs to Virtue and that We weakened our Political Economy to a point where Pride was able to slither its way into every aspect of our society.

Time will also declare whether We were willing and able to right ourselves. The evidence of our lives will close with our choices still to come.

Time will tell – if We chose to embrace Jefferson's "rightful liberty", if We chose Discernment and Reason over Ignorance and Stupidity, if We chose to turn our backs to Factions and the Monied Interests, if We chose to invest in our Knowledge and Character and Experience and Condition, if We chose to hoist Opportunity and Happiness onto their proper pedestal – if We decided to correct our course.

Finally, Time will see to it that We the People are forever picked apart forensically, our lives made available for study so that others may learn from our choices.

In Time, they will look at what We have done, either amazed by our dedication or disgusted by our lack thereof, awed by our devotion or disturbed by our destruction. They will read our words – either in admiration of our wisdom or contempt for our Hypocrisy. They will either celebrate how We put forth a positive example for the world or disown us as brethren of burden. They will look upon us as either sages or fools.

...we now stand in the vestibule of a vast new technological age – one that, despite its capacity for human destruction, has an equal capacity to make poverty and human misery obsolete. If our efforts are wisely directed – and if our unremitting efforts for dependable peace begin to attain some success – we can surely become participants in creating an age characterized by justice and rising levels of human well-being.[xiii]

– Dwight D. Eisenhower,
1960 State of the Union Address

---

xiii   Eisenhower, Dwight D. "1960 State of the Union Address." *Eisenhower Presidential Library, Museum, and Boyhood Home,* National Archives, 2021, www.eisenhowerlibrary.gov/.

Notes

1   Truman, Harry S., "Harry S. Truman Library and Museum." *Truman Library Institute*, https://www.trumanlibraryinstitute.org/truman/truman-quotes.

2   "To Thomas Jefferson from James Monroe, 17 June 1791," Founders Online, National Archives, https://founders.archives.gov/documents/Jefferson/01-20-02-0204. [Original source: The Papers of Thomas Jefferson, vol. 20, 1 April–4 August 1791, ed. Julian P. Boyd. Princeton: Princeton University Press, 1982, pp. 556–557.]

3   Jefferson, Thomas. "Thomas Jefferson to William Smith - Nov. 13. 1787." *Thomas Jefferson | Exhibitions - Library of Congress*, www.loc.gov/exhibits/jefferson/105.html.

4   "U.S. Constitution - Article I: Resources: Constitution Annotated: Congress.gov: Library of Congress." *Constitution Annotated*, constitution.congress.gov/constitution/article-1/.

5   "John Adams to Abigail Adams, 11 June 1775," *Founders Online*, National Archives, https://founders.archives.gov/documents/

Adams/04-01-02-0146. [Original source: *The Adams Papers*, Adams Family Correspondence, vol. 1, *December 1761–May 1776*, ed. Lyman H. Butterfield. Cambridge, MA: Harvard University Press, 1963, pp. 215–217.]

6   Madison, James. "Elliot's Debates: Volume 4." *Teaching American History*, teachingamericanhistory.org/resources/ratification/elliot/vol4/opinions/. *On the Establishment of a National Bank*. House of Representatives, *February 2, 1791*.

7   "From George Washington to the Pennsylvania Legislature, 12 September 1789," *Founders Online*, National Archives, https://founders.archives.gov/documents/Washington/05-04-02-0014. [Original source: *The Papers of George Washington*, Presidential Series, vol. 4, *8 September 1789–15 January 1790*, ed. Dorothy Twohig. Charlottesville: University Press of Virginia, 1993, pp. 23–25.]

8   "III. Thoughts on Government, April 1776," *Founders Online*, National Archives, https://founders.archives.gov/documents/Adams/06-04-02-0026-0004. [Original source: *The Adams Papers*, Papers of John Adams, vol. 4, *February–August 1776*, ed. Robert J. Taylor. Cambridge, MA: Harvard University Press, 1979, pp. 86–93.]

9   "Declaration of Independence, July 4, 1776," *National Archives*, https://www.archives.gov/founding-docs/declaration, *America's Founding Documents*, National Archives and Records Administration, 2020

10   Roosevelt, Theodore. "The Square Deal Speech" *AmericanLiter-ature*, https://americanliterature.com/history/theodore-roosevelt/speech/the-square-deal-speech, *The Square Deal Speech*, New York State Fair on Labor Day, *September 7, 1903*

11   Roosevelt, Franklin D. "The New Deal" *Pepperdine | School of Public Policy*, https://publicpolicy.pepperdine.edu/academics/research/faculty-research/new-deal/roosevelt-speeches/fr042938.htm/. *Message to Congress on the Concentration of Economic Power.* Congress of the United States, *April 29, 1938.*

12   E.B. & E.C. Kellogg , Printer. *"The people of these United States are the rightful masters of both congresses and courts, not to over-throw the Constitution, but to over-throw the men who pervert that Constitution" / E.B. & E.C. Kellogg, 245 Main Street, Hartford, Conn.* [New York: Geo. Whiting, 87 Fulton St] Photograph. Retrieved from the Library of Congress, <www.loc.gov/item/2008680376/>.

13   Washington, George. "Washington's Farewell Address 1796." *Avalon Project*, 2008 Lillian Goldman Law Library 127 Wall Street, New Haven, CT 06511., 2020, avalon.law.yale.edu/18th_century/washing.asp.

14   Washington, George. "Washington's Farewell Address 1796." *Avalon Project*, 2008 Lillian Goldman Law Library 127 Wall Street, New Haven, CT 06511., 2020, avalon.law.yale.edu/18th_century/washing.asp.

15   Washington, George. "From George Washington to John Armstrong, 26 March 1781." *Founders Online*, National Archives

and Records Administration, 2020, founders.archives.gov/documents/Washington/99-01-02-05206.

[16] Madison, James. "The Federalist Papers No. 57: The Alleged Tendency of the New Plan to Elevate the Few at the Expense of the Many Considered in Connection with Representation From the New York Packet. Tuesday, February 19, 1788." *Avalon Project*, 2008 Lillian Goldman Law Library 127 Wall Street, New Haven, CT 06511., 2020, avalon.law.yale.edu/18th_century/fed57.asp.

[17] "From John Adams to J. H. Tiffany, 31 March 1819," *Founders Online*, National Archives, https://founders.archives.gov/documents/Adams/99-02-02-7104. Source annotation: "This is an Early Access document from The Adams Papers. It is not an authoritative final version."

[18] Washington, George, 1792. *Outline of US Government*. Bureau of International Information Programs, U.S. Department of State, 2013. "Chapter 8 - GOVERNMENT OF THE PEOPLE, THE ROLE OF THE CITIZEN, The Media - page 124"

[19] Washington, George. "Letter to Major-General Robert Howe - Tuesday, August 17, 1779." *George Washington's Mount Vernon*, Mount Vernon Ladies' Association. All Rights Reserved., 2020, www.mountvernon.org/library/digitalhistory/quotes/article/few-men-have-virtue-to-withstand-the-highest-bidder/.

[20] Jackson, Andrew. "Andrew Jackson, May 27, 1830." *The Library of Congress*, 2020, www.loc.gov/item/maj025570/. Andrew Jackson Papers: Series 8, Messages and Speeches, Circa 1829 to 1836

21 "Nicomachean Ethics by Aristotle, Book II." Translated by W. D. Ross, *The Internet Classics Archive*, 1994-2009, Daniel C. Stevenson, Web Atomics, 2011, classics.mit.edu/Aristotle/nicomachaen.2.ii. html.

22 Jefferson, Thomas. "Thomas Jefferson to Horatio G. Spafford, 17 March 1814." *Founders Online*, National Archives and Records Administration, 2020, founders.archives.gov/documents/ Jefferson/03-07-02-0167.

23 Lincoln, Abraham. "State of the Union 1861." *American History From Revolution To Reconstruction and Beyond*, 1994-2012 GMW - University of Groningen, 2012, www.let.rug.nl/usa/presidents/ abraham-lincoln/state-of-the-union-1861.php.

24 Washington, George. "From George Washington to Benjamin Harrison, 10 October 1784." *Founders Online*, National Archives and Records Administration, 2020, https://founders.archives.gov/ documents/Washington/04-02-02-0082.

25 McKinley, William. "'Speeches and Addresses of William McKinley, from His Election to Congress to the Present Time.'" *Internet Archive*, The Internet Archive, 2020, archive.org/stream/ speechesaddresse01mcki/speechesaddresse01mcki_djvu.txt. Page 376.

26 Monroe, James. "March 4, 1817: First Inaugural Address." *Miller Center*, 2019. Rector and Visitors of the University of Virginia, 23 Feb. 2017, millercenter.org/the-presidency/presidential-speeches/ march-4-1817-first-inaugural-address.

27 "From John Adams to John Taylor, 17 December 1814," *Founders Online*, National Archives, https://founders.archives. gov/documents/Adams/99-02-02-6371. [This is an Early Access document from The Adams Papers. It is not an authoritative final version.]

28 "From John Adams to Boston Patriot, 4 August 1809," *Founders Online*, National Archives, https://founders.archives. gov/documents/Adams/99-02-02-5405. [This is an Early Access document from The Adams Papers. It is not an authoritative final version.]

29 "Washington, George. "Washington's Farewell Address 1796." *Avalon Project*, 2008 Lillian Goldman Law Library 127 Wall Street, New Haven, CT 06511., 2020, avalon.law.yale.edu/18th_century/ washing.asp.

30 "From George Washington to Major General Philip Schuyler, 15 July 1777," *Founders Online*, National Archives, https://founders. archives.gov/documents/Washington/03-10-02-0282. [Original source: *The Papers of George Washington*, Revolutionary War Series, vol. 10, *11 June 1777–18 August 1777*, ed. Frank E. Grizzard, Jr. Charlottesville: University Press of Virginia, 2000, pp. 289–291.]

31 Meyers, Robert Cornelius V. "Theodore Roosevelt, Patriot and Statesman: The True Story of an Ideal American." *Google Books*, P. W. Ziegler & Company [c1902], books.google.com/ books?id=kfYEAAAAYAAJ. Page 521

³² "Addresses of President Wilson, January 27-February 3, 1916." *Google Books*, House of Representatives, 3 Feb. 1916, www.google.com/books/edition/Addresses_of_President_Wilson_January_27/8_NHAQAAMAAJ?hl=en. Page 13

33 "From John Adams to John Taylor, 15 April 1814," *Founders Online*, National Archives, https://founders.archives.gov/documents/Adams/99-02-02-6278. [This is an Early Access document from The Adams Papers. It is not an authoritative final version.]

³⁴ "Nicomachean Ethics by Aristotle, Book I." Translated by W. D. Ross, *The Internet Classics Archive*, 1994-2009, Daniel C. Stevenson, Web Atomics, 2011, classics.mit.edu/Aristotle/nicomachaen.2.ii.html.

³⁵ "Nicomachean Ethics by Aristotle, Book II." Translated by W. D. Ross, *The Internet Classics Archive*, 1994-2009, Daniel C. Stevenson, Web Atomics, 2011, classics.mit.edu/Aristotle/nicomachaen.2.ii.html.

³⁶ Roosevelt, Theodore. "Letter from Theodore Roosevelt to S. Stanwood Menken, 10 January 1917." *Theodore Roosevelt Center*, Theodore Roosevelt Digital Library. Dickinson State University., 2020, www.theodorerooseveltcenter.org/Research/Digital-Library/Record?libID=o280589. [Original Source: *Theodore Roosevelt Collection*. MS Am 1785.2 (107). Harvard College Library.]

³⁷ "From John Adams to Mercy Otis Warren, 16 April 1776," *Founders Online*, National Archives, https://founders.archives.gov/

documents/Adams/06-04-02-0044. [Original source: *The Adams Papers*, Papers of John Adams, vol. 4, *February–August 1776*, ed. Robert J. Taylor. Cambridge, MA: Harvard University Press, 1979, pp. 123–126.]

[38] "From George Washington to Alexander Hamilton, 26 August 1792," *Founders Online*, National Archives, https://founders.archives.gov/documents/Washington/05-11-02-0015. [Original source: *The Papers of George Washington*, Presidential Series, vol. 11, *16 August 1792–15 January 1793*, ed. Christine Sternberg Patrick. Charlottesville: University of Virginia Press, 2002, pp. 38–40.]

[39] Contributors to Wikimedia. "William McKinley, 25th President of the United States (in Office from 1897 to 1901)." *Wikiquote*, Wikimedia Foundation, Inc., 20 Dec. 2020, en.wikiquote.org/wiki/William_McKinley. While these words are widely attributed to President McKinley, as of the date of this publishing this author has not verified the precise source.

[40] "III. First Inaugural Address, 4 March 1801," *Founders Online*, National Archives, https://founders.archives.gov/documents/Jefferson/01-33-02-0116-0004. [Original source: *The Papers of Thomas Jefferson*, vol. 33, *17 February–30 April 1801*, ed. Barbara B. Oberg. Princeton: Princeton University Press, 2006, pp. 148–152.]

[41] Jefferson, Thomas. "The Life and Writings of Thomas Jefferson." *Google Books*, Bowen-Merrill Company, 1900, books.google.com/books?id=niMWAAAAYAAJ. Page 136. [Original Source: *Notes on Virginia*, 1782.]

42   United States, and American Imprint Collection. *We the people of the United States, in order to form a more perfect union, establish justice, insure domestic tranquility, provide for the common defence, promote the general welfare, and secure the blessings of liberty to ourselves and our posterity, do ordain and establish this constitution for the United States of America.* [Philadelphia: Printed by Dunlap & Claypoole, 1787] Online Text. Retrieved from the Library of Congress, <www.loc.gov/item/48034353/>.

43   Nicomachean Ethics by Aristotle, Book II." Translated by W. D. Ross, *The Internet Classics Archive*, 1994-2009, Daniel C. Stevenson, Web Atomics, 2011, classics.mit.edu/Aristotle/nicomachaen.2.ii.html.

44   Thayer, William M. "From Log-Cabin to White House: The Story of President Garfield's Life." *Google Books*, Hodder and Stoughton, 1884, books.google.com/books?id=pUUIAAAAQAAJ. Page 208

45   Lincoln, Abraham. "Address before the Wisconsin State Agricultural Society." *Abraham Lincoln Online*, 2018 Abraham Lincoln Online, 2018, http://www.abrahamlincolnonline.org/lincoln/speeches/fair.htm. September 30, 1859. Milwaukee, Wisconsin.. Source: Collected Works of Abraham Lincoln, edited by Roy P. Basler et al.

46   "Thomas Jefferson to John Wayles Eppes, 6 November 1813," *Founders Online*, National Archives, https://founders.archives.gov/documents/Jefferson/03-06-02-0458. [Original source: *The Papers of Thomas Jefferson*, Retirement Series, vol. 6, *11 March to*

27 November 1813, ed. J. Jefferson Looney. Princeton: Princeton University Press, 2009, pp. 578–594.]

[47]   *Facts for workingmen. More has been done in the interest of labor, by legislation, in the state of New York, within the past two years, than was ever done before in the history of the state* ... Vote for Grover Cleveland for the presidency ... n. 1884. Pdf. Retrieved from the Library of Congress, <www.loc.gov/item/rbpe.23802500/>.

[48]   Roosevelt, Franklin D. "July 8, 1938: Dedication of a Memorial to the Northwest Territory." *Miller Center*, 2019. Rector and Visitors of the University of Virginia, 26 April 2017, https://millercenter.org/the-presidency/presidential-speeches/july-8-1938-dedication-memorial-northwest-territory.

[49]   Adams, John. "The Works of John Adams Vol. 6." *Google Books*, Jazzybee Verlag, 20 Apr. 2017, www.google.com/books/edition/The_Works_of_John_Adams_Vol_6/UQm0DgAAQBAJ?hl=en. Page 158

[50]   Garfield, James. "The Works of James Abram Garfield. Volume 2, 1882." *Google Books*, Best Books On, www.google.com/books/edition/The_works_of_James_Abram_Garfield_Volume/8gv5AwAAQBAJ?hl=en. Page 486

[51]   "From George Washington to David Humphreys, 8 March 1787," *Founders Online*, National Archives, https://founders.archives.gov/documents/Washington/04-05-02-0071.   [Original source: *The Papers of George Washington*, Confederation Series,

vol. 5, *1 February 1787–31 December 1787*, ed. W. W. Abbot. Charlottesville: University Press of Virginia, 1997, pp. 72–73.]

52   Lincoln, Abraham. "Lyceum Address." *Abraham Lincoln Online*, 2018 Abraham Lincoln Online, www.abrahamlincolnonline.org/lincoln/speeches/lyceum.htm. *The Perpetuation of Our Political Institutions: Address Before the Young Men's Lyceum of Springfield, Illinois. January 27, 1838* [Source: Collected Works of Abraham Lincoln, edited by Roy P. Basler et al.]

53   Lincoln, Abraham. "Annual Message to Congress – Concluding Remarks." *Abraham Lincoln Online*, 2020 Abraham Lincoln Online, http://www.abrahamlincolnonline.org/lincoln/speeches/congress.htm. Washington, D.C. December 1, 1862 [Source: Collected Works of Abraham Lincoln, edited by Roy P. Basler et al.]

54   Roosevelt, Theodore. "Theodore Roosevelt: His Life and Times on Film : Progressive Covenant with the People." *The Library of Congress*, Congress.gov, 2020, www.loc.gov/collections/theodore-roosevelt-films/articles-and-essays/sound-recordings-of-theodore-roosevelts-voice/.

55   "Thomas Jefferson to Isaac H. Tiffany, 4 April 1819," *Founders Online*, National Archives, https://founders.archives.gov/documents/Jefferson/03-14-02-0191. [Original source: *The Papers of Thomas Jefferson*, Retirement Series, vol. 14, *1 February to 31 August 1819*, ed. J. Jefferson Looney. Princeton: Princeton University Press, 2017, pp. 201–202.]

[56] "From John Adams to Thomas Jefferson, 2 February 1816," *Founders Online*, National Archives, https://founders.archives.gov/documents/Adams/99-02-02-6575. [This is an Early Access document from *The Adams Papers*. It is not an authoritative final version.]

[57] "Thomas Jefferson to George Logan, 12 November 1816," *Founders Online*, National Archives, https://founders.archives.gov/documents/Jefferson/03-10-02-0390. [Original source: *The Papers of Thomas Jefferson*, Retirement Series, vol. 10, *May 1816 to 18 January 1817*, ed. J. Jefferson Looney. Princeton: Princeton University Press, 2013, pp. 521–522.]

[58] Roosevelt, Theodore. "'Presidential Addresses and State Paper, April 7, 1904 to May 9, 1905.'" *Internet Archive*, The Internet Archive, 2020, https://archive.org/details/presidentialadd15roosrich. Page 321. [Original source: The Review of Reviews Company, 1910]

[59] Madison, James. "James Madison to W. T. Barry, August 4, 1822." Manuscript/Mixed Material. *Library of Congress*, https://www.loc.gov/resource/mjm.20_0155_0159/?sp=1&st=text.

[60] Smith, Adam. "An Inquiry into the Nature and Causes of the Wealth of Nations, Book I Chapter II, Of the Principle Which Gives Occasion to the Division of Labour, 1776." *Project Gutenberg*, EBook of An Inquiry into the Nature and Causes of the Wealth of Nations, 17 September 2019, https://www.gutenberg.org/files/3300/3300-h/3300-h.htm. Salt Lake City, UT. [Original Publisher: W. Strahan and T. Cadell, London, 1776]

61   Smith, Adam. "Theory of Moral Sentiments, Part IV. Of the Effect of Utility upon the Sentiment of Approbation, Chapter 1: The beauty that the appearance of utility gives to all the productions of art, and the widespread influence of this type of beauty, 1759." *Econlib : The Library of Economics and Liberty*, Liberty Fund, Inc., 2019, www.econlib.org/book-chapters/chapter-part-iv-of-the-effect-of-utility-upon-the-sentiment-of-approbation/.

62   "Thomas Jefferson to Charles Yancey, 6 January 1816," *Founders Online*, National Archives, https://founders.archives.gov/documents/Jefferson/03-09-02-0209. [Original source: *The Papers of Thomas Jefferson*, Retirement Series, vol. 9, *September 1815 to April 1816*, ed. J. Jefferson Looney. Princeton: Princeton University Press, 2012, pp. 328–331.]

63   Lincoln, Abraham. "Lyceum Address." Abraham Lincoln Online, 2018 Abraham Lincoln Online, www.abrahamlincolnonline.org/lincoln/speeches/lyceum.htm. The Perpetuation of Our Political Institutions: Address Before the Young Men's Lyceum of Springfield, Illinois. January 27, 1838 [Source: Collected Works of Abraham Lincoln, edited by Roy P. Basler et al.]

64   Riddle, Albert G. "The Life, Character and Public Services of Jas. A. Garfield, 1880." *Google Books*, W.W. Williams, 1881, https://www.google.com/books/edition/The_Life_Character_and_Public_Services_o/SsHthaAe0CwC?hl=en&gbpv=0. Pages 382-383

65   Nicomachean Ethics by Aristotle, Book I." Translated by W. D. Ross, *The Internet Classics Archive*, 1994-2009, Daniel

C. Stevenson, Web Atomics, 2011, classics.mit.edu/Aristotle/nicomachaen.1.i.html.

⁶⁶ Politics by Aristotle, 350 B.C.E, Book Seven." Translated by Benjamin Jowett, *The Internet Classics Archive*, 1994-2009, Daniel C. Stevenson, Web Atomics, 2011, http://classics.mit.edu/Aristotle/politics.7.seven.html.

⁶⁷ Roosevelt, Theodore. "Theodore Roosevelt Quotes." *Theodore Roosevelt Center*, Dickinson State University, 2020, www.theodorerooseveltcenter.org/Quote-of-the-Day?page=75. Source Annotation: Roosevelt wrote these words in the Forum in January 1897. He was quick to note that he did not think the United States was on the road to dissolution, but he was certain that we needed to tone up our national manliness. A little more than a year later, he would lead the charge up Kettle and San Juan hills in Cuba.

⁶⁸ Lincoln, Abraham. "Lyceum Address." *Abraham Lincoln Online*, 2018 Abraham Lincoln Online, www.abrahamlincolnonline.org/lincoln/speeches/lyceum.htm. *The Perpetuation of Our Political Institutions: Address Before the Young Men's Lyceum of Springfield, Illinois. January 27, 1838* [Source: Collected Works of Abraham Lincoln, edited by Roy P. Basler et al.]

⁶⁹ Lincoln, Abraham. "First Political Announcement, 1832" *Abraham Lincoln Online*, 2020 Abraham Lincoln Online, http://www.abrahamlincolnonline.org/lincoln/speeches/1832.htm. First Political Announcement: *To the People of Sangamo County, New Salem, Illinois, March 9, 1832* [Source: Collected Works of Abraham Lincoln, edited by Roy P. Basler et al.]

70   "From James Madison to William T. Barry, 4 August 1822," Founders Online, National Archives, https://founders.archives. gov/documents/Madison/04-02-02-0480. [Original source: The Papers of James Madison, Retirement Series, vol. 2, 1 February 1820–26 February 1823, ed. David B. Mattern, J. C. A. Stagg, Mary Parke Johnson, and Anne Mandeville Colony. Charlottesville: University of Virginia Press, 2013, pp. 555–558.]

71   McKinley, William. "Papers Relating to the Foreign Relations of the United States, with the Annual Message of the President Transmitted to Congress December 5, 1899." *Office of the Historian, Foreign Service Institute United States Department of State*, U.S. Department of State, 2020, history.state.gov/historicaldocuments/ frus1899/message-of-the-president.

72   Smith, Adam. "An Inquiry into the Nature and Causes of the Wealth of Nations, Book II Chapter I, Of the Division of Stock, 1776." *Project Gutenberg*, EBook of An Inquiry into the Nature and Causes of the Wealth of Nations, 17 September 2019, https://www. gutenberg.org/files/3300/3300-h/3300-h.htm. Salt Lake City, UT. [Original Publisher: W. Strahan and T. Cadell, London, 1776]

73   Smith, Adam. "An Inquiry into the Nature and Causes of the Wealth of Nations, Book II Chapter III, Of the Accumulation of Capital, or Of Productive and Unproductive Labour, 1776." *Project Gutenberg*, EBook of An Inquiry into the Nature and Causes of the Wealth of Nations, 17 September 2019, https://www.gutenberg. org/files/3300/3300-h/3300-h.htm. Salt Lake City, UT. [Original Publisher: W. Strahan and T. Cadell, London, 1776]

74 "James Madison to Littleton Dennis Teackle, 29 March 1826," *Founders Online*, National Archives, https://founders.archives. gov/documents/Madison/99-02-02-0646. [This is an Early Access document from The Papers of James Madison. It is not an authoritative final version.]

75 Roosevelt, Franklin D. "Franklin D. Roosevelt Speeches: Oglethorpe University Address, The New Deal, 22 May 1932" *Pepperdine | School of Public Policy*, 2021 Pepperdine University, https://publicpolicy.pepperdine.edu/academics/research/faculty-research/new-deal/roosevelt-speeches/fr052232.htm.

76 "From George Washington to George Chapman, 15 December 1784," *Founders Online*, National Archives, https://founders. archives.gov/documents/Washington/04-02-02-0149. [Original source: *The Papers of George Washington*, Confederation Series, vol. 2, *18 July 1784–18 May 1785*, ed. W. W. Abbot. Charlottesville: University Press of Virginia, 1992, pp. 183–184.]

77 "Washington, George. "First Annual Message of George Washington, 1790." *Avalon Project*, 2008 Lillian Goldman Law Library 127 Wall Street, New Haven, CT 06511., https://avalon. law.yale.edu/18th_century/washs01.asp. [Source: *A Compilation of the Messages and Papers of the Presidents*, Prepared under the direction of the Joint Committee on printing, of the House and Senate, Pursuant to an Act of the Fifty-Second Congress of the United States. New York : Bureau of National Literature, Inc., 1897]

78 "From George Washington to James Anderson, 21 December 1797," *Founders Online*, National Archives, https://founders.

archives.gov/documents/Washington/06-01-02-0465.   [Original source: *The Papers of George Washington*, Retirement Series, vol. 1, *4 March 1797–30 December 1797*, ed. W. W. Abbot. Charlottesville: University Press of Virginia, 1998, pp. 523–527.]

79   The Republic by Plato, 360 B.C.E, Book II." Translated by Benjamin Jowett, The Internet Classics Archive, 1994-2009, Daniel C. Stevenson, Web Atomics, 2011, http://classics.mit.edu/Plato/republic.3.ii.html.

80   Smith, Adam. "An Inquiry into the Nature and Causes of the Wealth of Nations, Book I Chapter I, Of The Division of Labour, 1776." *Project Gutenberg*, EBook of An Inquiry into the Nature and Causes of the Wealth of Nations, 17 September 2019, https://www.gutenberg.org/files/3300/3300-h/3300-h.htm. Salt Lake City, UT. [Original Publisher: W. Strahan and T. Cadell, London, 1776]

81   Smith, Adam. "An Inquiry into the Nature and Causes of the Wealth of Nations, Book I Chapter II, Of The Principle Which Gives Occasion to The Division of Labour, 1776." *Project Gutenberg*, EBook of An Inquiry into the Nature and Causes of the Wealth of Nations, 17 September 2019, https://www.gutenberg.org/files/3300/3300-h/3300-h.htm. Salt Lake City, UT. [Original Publisher: W. Strahan and T. Cadell, London, 1776]

82   Smith, Adam. "An Inquiry into the Nature and Causes of the Wealth of Nations, Book I Chapter X, Of Wages And Profit In The Different Employments Of Labour And Stock, 1776." *Project Gutenberg*, EBook of An Inquiry into the Nature and Causes of the Wealth of Nations, 17 September 2019, https://www.gutenberg.

org/files/3300/3300-h/3300-h.htm. Salt Lake City, UT. [Original Publisher: W. Strahan and T. Cadell, London, 1776]

83   "From George Washington to Daniel Morgan, 8 October 1794," *Founders Online*, National Archives, https://founders.archives. gov/documents/Washington/05-17-02-0024. [Original source: *The Papers of George Washington*, Presidential Series, vol. 17, *1 October 1794–31 March 1795*, ed. David R. Hoth and Carol S. Ebel. Charlottesville: University of Virginia Press, 2013, pp. 39–40.]

84   Smith, Adam. "An Inquiry into the Nature and Causes of the Wealth of Nations, Book IV Chapter II, Of Restraints Upon Importation From Foreign Countries Of Such Goods As Can Be Produced At Home, 1776." *Project Gutenberg*, EBook of An Inquiry into the Nature and Causes of the Wealth of Nations, 17 September 2019, https://www.gutenberg.org/files/3300/3300-h/3300-h.htm. Salt Lake City, UT. [Original Publisher: W. Strahan and T. Cadell, London, 1776]

85   "To Thomas Jefferson from John Adams, 25 August 1787," *Founders Online*, National Archives, https://founders.archives. gov/documents/Jefferson/01-12-02-0064. [Original source: *The Papers of Thomas Jefferson*, vol. 12, *7 August 1787–31 March 1788*, ed. Julian P. Boyd. Princeton: Princeton University Press, 1955, pp. 55–56.]

86   Smith, Adam. "An Inquiry into the Nature and Causes of the Wealth of Nations, Book II Chapter III, Of The Accumulation of Capital, Or Of Productive And Unproductive Labour, 1776." *Project Gutenberg*, EBook of An Inquiry into the Nature and Causes of the

Wealth of Nations, 17 September 2019, https://www.gutenberg.org/files/3300/3300-h/3300-h.htm. Salt Lake City, UT. [Original Publisher: W. Strahan and T. Cadell, London, 1776]

87   Smith, Adam. "An Inquiry into the Nature and Causes of the Wealth of Nations, Book II Chapter III, Of The Accumulation of Capital, Or Of Productive And Unproductive Labour, 1776." *Project Gutenberg*, EBook of An Inquiry into the Nature and Causes of the Wealth of Nations, 17 September 2019, https://www.gutenberg.org/files/3300/3300-h/3300-h.htm. Salt Lake City, UT. [Original Publisher: W. Strahan and T. Cadell, London, 1776]

88   Smith, Adam. "An Inquiry into the Nature and Causes of the Wealth of Nations, Book II Chapter III, Of The Accumulation of Capital, Or Of Productive And Unproductive Labour, 1776." *Project Gutenberg*, EBook of An Inquiry into the Nature and Causes of the Wealth of Nations, 17 September 2019, https://www.gutenberg.org/files/3300/3300-h/3300-h.htm. Salt Lake City, UT. [Original Publisher: W. Strahan and T. Cadell, London, 1776]

89   Smith, Adam. "An Inquiry into the Nature and Causes of the Wealth of Nations, Book II Chapter III, Of The Accumulation of Capital, Or Of Productive And Unproductive Labour, 1776." *Project Gutenberg*, EBook of An Inquiry into the Nature and Causes of the Wealth of Nations, 17 September 2019, https://www.gutenberg.org/files/3300/3300-h/3300-h.htm. Salt Lake City, UT. [Original Publisher: W. Strahan and T. Cadell, London, 1776]

90   Smith, Adam. "An Inquiry into the Nature and Causes of the Wealth of Nations, Book II Chapter III, Of The Accumulation of

Capital, Or Of Productive And Unproductive Labour, 1776." *Project Gutenberg*, EBook of An Inquiry into the Nature and Causes of the Wealth of Nations, 17 September 2019, https://www.gutenberg.org/files/3300/3300-h/3300-h.htm. Salt Lake City, UT. [Original Publisher: W. Strahan and T. Cadell, London, 1776]

[91]   Smith, Adam. "An Inquiry into the Nature and Causes of the Wealth of Nations, Book II Chapter III, Of The Accumulation of Capital, Or Of Productive And Unproductive Labour, 1776." *Project Gutenberg*, EBook of An Inquiry into the Nature and Causes of the Wealth of Nations, 17 September 2019, https://www.gutenberg.org/files/3300/3300-h/3300-h.htm. Salt Lake City, UT. [Original Publisher: W. Strahan and T. Cadell, London, 1776]

[92]   Lazarus, Emma. "The New Colossus, 1883." *Statue of Liberty*, National Parks Service, U.S. Department of the Interior, 14 Aug. 2019, www.nps.gov/stli/learn/historyculture/colossus.htm. [Addition Information: 2020 Poetry Foundation, https://www.poetryfoundation.org/poets/emma-lazarus, *Emma Lazarus* 1849–1887. "Lines from that 1883 sonnet, "The New Colossus," were engraved on the pedestal of the Statue of Liberty in 1903."]

[93]   "From Thomas Jefferson to Columbia, South Carolina, Citizens, 23 March 1801," *Founders Online*, National Archives, https://founders.archives.gov/documents/Jefferson/01-33-02-0350.
[Original source: *The Papers of Thomas Jefferson*, vol. 33, *17 February–30 April 1801*, ed. Barbara B. Oberg. Princeton: Princeton University Press, 2006, p. 409.]

94   Marx, Karl. "Wage-Labour and Capital, 1849." *Google Books*, Wildside Press LLC, 1 Apr. 2008, books.google.com/books?id=RX9irx0oI64C. Page 43

95   Cleveland, Grover. "State of the Union Address, December 3, 1888." *Teaching American History*, https://teachingamericanhistory.org/library/document/state-of-the-union-address-89/.

96   "From John Adams to John Taylor, 17 December 1814," *Founders Online*, National Archives, https://founders.archives.gov/documents/Adams/99-02-02-6371. [This is an Early Access document from The Adams Papers. It is not an authoritative final version.]

97   "The Pledge of Allegiance." *Ushistory.org*, Independence Hall Association, 2019, www.ushistory.org/documents/pledge.htm?vm=r. [Independence Hall Association notation: "The Pledge of Allegiance was written in August 1892 by the socialist minister Francis Bellamy (1855-1931). It was originally published in *The Youth's Companion* on September 8, 1892. Bellamy had hoped that the pledge would be used by citizens in any country. In its original form it read: 'I pledge allegiance to my Flag and the Republic for which it stands, one nation, indivisible, with liberty and justice for all.'"]

98   Wilson, Woodrow. "First Inaugural Address of Woodrow Wilson, Tuesday, March 4, 1913." *Avalon Project*, 2008 Lillian Goldman Law Library 127 Wall Street, New Haven, CT 06511., 2020, https://avalon.law.yale.edu/20th_century/wilson1.asp.

99   Lincoln, Abraham. "Seventh Debate with Douglas, October 15, 1858." *House Divided Project*, Matthew Pinsker, Editor. Dickinson

State University., 2020, http://housedivided.dickinson.edu/sites/lincoln/seventh-debate-with-douglas-october-15-1858/.

100 "John Adams to Thomas Jefferson, 24 August 1815," *Founders Online*, National Archives, https://founders.archives.gov/documents/Jefferson/03-08-02-0560. [Original source: *The Papers of Thomas Jefferson*, Retirement Series, vol. 8, *1 October 1814 to 31 August 1815*, ed. J. Jefferson Looney. Princeton: Princeton University Press, 2011, pp. 682–684.]

101 Lincoln, Abraham. "The Gettysburg Address, November 19, 1863" *Abraham Lincoln Online*, 2020 Abraham Lincoln Online, http://www.abrahamlincolnonline.org/lincoln/speeches/gettysburg.htm. Gettysburg, Pennsylvania [Source: Collected Works of Abraham Lincoln, edited by Roy P. Basler et al.]

102 "The Liberty Bell." Independence National Historical Park, *National Parks Service*, U.S. Department of the Interior, 2020, https://www.nps.gov/inde/learn/historyculture/stories-libertybell.htm. [National Parks Service notation: "The Liberty Bell's inscription is from the Bible (King James version): 'Proclaim Liberty Throughout All the Land Unto All the Inhabitants thereof.'"]

103 Lincoln, Abraham. "The Gettysburg Address, November 19, 1863" *Abraham Lincoln Online*, 2020 Abraham Lincoln Online, http://www.abrahamlincolnonline.org/lincoln/speeches/gettysburg.htm. Gettysburg, Pennsylvania [Source: Collected Works of Abraham Lincoln, edited by Roy P. Basler et al.]